SHETAUT NETER

Daily
Chant, Songbook,
Meditation and
Devotional Worship Manual

by
Sebai Dr. Muata Abhaya Ashby

On the cover: Queen Nefertary makes offering to the Divine.

Sema (𓊃) is an ancient Egyptian word and symbol meaning *union*. The Sema Institute is dedicated to the propagation of the universal teachings of spiritual evolution which relate to the union of humanity and the union of all things within the universe. Our primary goals are to provide the wisdom of ancient spiritual teachings in books, courses and other forms of communication. Secondly, to provide expert instruction and training in the various yogic disciplines including Ancient Egyptian Philosophy, Christian Gnosticism, Indian Philosophy and modern science. Thirdly, to promote world peace and Universal Love. A primary focus of our tradition is to identify and acknowledge the yogic principles within all religions and to relate them to each other in order to promote their deeper understanding as well as to show the essential unity of purpose and the unity of all living beings and nature within the whole of existence. The Institute is open to all who believe in the principles of peace, non-violence and spiritual emancipation regardless of sex, race, or creed.

Cruzian Mystic Books

P.O.Box 570459
Miami, Florida, 33257
(305) 378-6253 Fax: (305) 378-6253

First U.S. edition 1997

© 1999 By Muata Abhaya Ashby

© 2001 By Muata Abhaya Ashby 5-01

© 2003 By Muata Abhaya Ashby 9-03

© 2006 By Muata Abhaya Ashby 11-06

The author is available for group lectures and individual counseling. For further information contact the publisher.

Ashby, Muata
The Devotional Worship Book of Shetaut Neter: The daily Chant,Pprayer and Songbook of the Ancient Egyptian Mysteries ISBN: 1-884564-32-1

1 Egyptian Mythology 2 Spirituality 3 Religion 4 Yoga 5 Self Help.

About Sebai Muata Ashby

Sebai Dr. Muata Abhaya Ashby is a Priest of Shetaut Neter –African Kamitan Religion, Author, lecturer, poet, philosopher, musician, publisher, counselor and spiritual preceptor and founder of the Sema Institute-Temple of Aset, Muata Ashby was born in Brooklyn, New York City, and grew up in the Caribbean. His family is from Puerto Rico and Barbados. Displaying an interest in ancient civilizations and the Humanities, Sebai Maa began studies in the area of religion and philosophy and achieved doctorates in these areas while at the same time he began to collect his research into what would later become several books on the subject of the origins of Yoga Philosophy and practice in ancient Africa (Ancient Egypt) and also the origins of Christian Mysticism in Ancient Egypt.

Sebai Maa (Muata Abhaya Ashby) holds a Doctor of Divinity Degree in Holistic Health and a Masters degree in Liberal Arts and Religious Studies. He is a certified member of the American Alternative Medical Associations an Alternative Medical Practitioner. He is also a Pastoral Counselor and Teacher of Yoga Philosophy and Discipline. Dr. Ashby received his Doctor of Divinity Degree from and is an adjunct faculty member of Florida International university and the American Institute of Holistic Theology. Dr. Ashby is a certified as a PREP Relationship Counselor. Dr. Ashby has been an independent researcher and practitioner of Egyptian Yoga, Indian Yoga, Chinese Yoga, Buddhism and mystical psychology as well as Christian Mysticism. He has extensively studied mystical religious traditions from around the world and is an accomplished lecturer, musician, artist, poet, screenwriter, playwright and author of over 35 books on Kemetic yoga and spiritual philosophy. He is an Ordained Minister and Spiritual Counselor and also the founder the Sema Institute, a non-profit organization dedicated to spreading the wisdom of Yoga and the Ancient Egyptian mystical traditions. Further, he is the spiritual leader and head priest of the Per Aset or Temple of Aset, based in Miami, Florida. Thus, as a scholar, Dr. Muata Ashby is a teacher, lecturer and researcher. However, as a spiritual leader, his title is *Sebai,* which means Spiritual Preceptor.

Table of Contents

INTRODUCTION TO NETERIANISM AND DIVINE WORSHIP

The Fundamental Principles of Ancient Egyptian Religion

NETERIANISM
(The Oldest Known Religion in History)

The term "Neterianism" is derived from the name "Shetaut Neter." Shetaut Neter means the "Hidden Divinity." It is the ancient philosophy and mythic spiritual culture that gave rise to the Ancient Egyptian civilization. Those who follow the spiritual path of Shetaut Neter are therefore referred to as "Neterians." The fundamental principles of Ancient Egyptian Religion may be summed up in four "Great Truths" that are common to all the traditions of Ancient Egyptian Religion.

The Spiritual Culture and the Purpose of Life: Shetaut Neter

"Men and women are to become God-like
through a life of virtue and the cultivation of
the spirit through scientific knowledge,
practice and bodily discipline."

-Ancient Egyptian Proverb

The highest forms of Joy, Peace and Contentment are obtained when the meaning of life is discovered. When the human being is in harmony with life, then it is possible to reflect and meditate upon the human condition and realize the limitations of worldly pursuits. When there is peace and harmony in life, a human being can practice any of the varied disciplines designated as Shetaut Neter to promote {his/her} evolution towards the ultimate goal of life, which Spiritual Enlightenment. Spiritual Enlightenment is the awakening of a human being to the awareness of the Transcendental essence which binds the universe and which is eternal and immutable. In this discovery is also the sobering and ecstatic realization that the human being is one with that Transcendental essence. With this realization comes great joy, peace and power to experience the fullness of life and to realize the purpose of life during the time on earth. The lotus is a symbol of Shetaut Neter, meaning the turning towards the light of truth, peace and transcendental harmony.

Fundamental Principles of Shetaut Neter African Religion

What is Shetaut Neter? The Ancient Egyptians were African peoples who lived in the north-eastern quadrant of the continent of Africa. They were descendants of the Nubians, who had themselves originated from farther south into the heart of Africa at the great lakes region, the sources of the Nile River. They created a vast civilization and culture earlier than any other society in known history and organized a nation which was based on the concepts of balance and order as well as spiritual enlightenment. These ancient African people called their land Kamit and soon after developing a well ordered society they began to realize that the world is full of wonders but life is fleeting and that there must be something more to human existence. They developed spiritual systems that were designed to allow human beings to understand the nature of this secret being who is the essence of all Creation. They called this spiritual system "Shtaut Ntr."

Definitions:

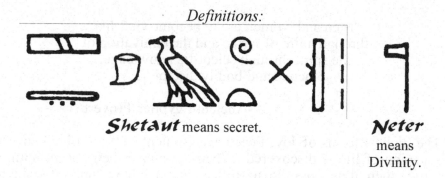

Shetaut means secret. **Neter** means Divinity.

The Religion of Ancient Kamit (Egypt) is *Neterianism*. The terms "Shetaut Neter" and "Neterianism" will be used interchangeably throughout this work.

SHETAUT NETER (NETERIANISM), A RELIGION OF ANCIENT AFRICA

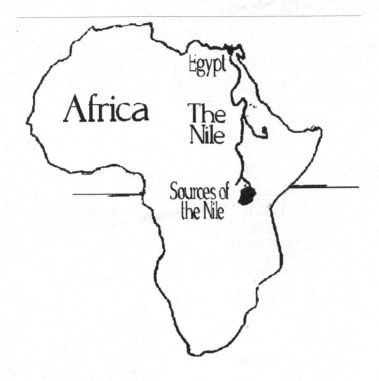

The Origin of the Term Shetaut

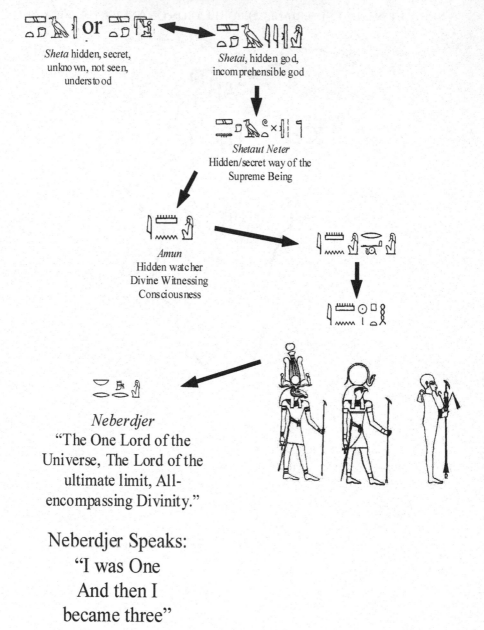

Sheta hidden, secret, unknown, not seen, understood

Shetai, hidden god, incomprehensible god

Shetaut Neter
Hidden/secret way of the Supreme Being

Amun
Hidden watcher
Divine Witnessing
Consciousness

Neberdjer
"The One Lord of the Universe, The Lord of the ultimate limit, All-encompassing Divinity."

Neberdjer Speaks:
"I was One
And then I
became three"

The term "Shetaut" has its root in the term Sheta which means "hidden" or "Secret," i.e. a mystery. The Divine (Neter) is a mystery because it is hidden from the physical senses and the simple-minded personality. So religion is the study of the hidden Divinity (Shetaut Neter, lit. hidden Divine Self). The term Amun also means Hidden. Amun is the first aspect in a Triune manifestation of spirit (Amun-Ra_Ptah) which emanates from the "All-Encompassing" Divinity called "Neberdger."

Who is Neter?

"Ntr"

Who is Ntr?

The symbol of Neter was described by an Ancient Kamitan sage as:

"That which is placed in the coffin"

The term Ntr, or Ntjr, come from the Ancient Egyptian hieroglyphic language which did not record its vowels. However, the term survives in the Coptic language as *"Nutar."* The same Coptic meaning (divine force or sustaining power) applies in the present as it did in ancient times, It is a symbol composed of a wooden staff that was wrapped with strips of fabric, like a mummy. The strips alternate in color with yellow, green and blue. The mummy in Kamitan spirituality is understood to be the dead but resurrected Divinity. So the Nutar is actually every human being who does not really die, but goes to live on in a different form. Further, the resurrected spirit of every human being is that same Divinity. Phonetically, the term Nutar is related to other terms having the same meaning, the latin "Natura," Spanish Naturalesa, English "Nature" and

"Nutriment", etc. In a real sense, as we will see, Natur means power manifesting as Neteru and the Neteru are the objects of creation, i.e. "nature."

The Follower of Neterianism

"Shemsu Neter"

"Follower (of) Neter"

The term "Neterianism" is derived from the name "Shetaut Neter." Those who follow the spiritual path of Shetaut Neter are therefore referred to as "Neterians."

Neterianism is the science of Neter, that is, the study of the secret or mystery of Neter, the enigma of that which transcends ordinary consciousness but from which all creation arises. The world did not come from nothing, nor is it sustained by nothing. Rather it is a manifestation of that which is beyond time and space but which at the same time permeates and maintains the fundamental elements. In other words, it is the substratum of Creation and the essential nature of all that exists.

So those who follow the Neter may be referred to as Neterians.

The fundamental principles common to all denominations of Ancient Egyptian (African) Religion may be summed up in four "Great Truths" that are common to all the traditions of Ancient Egyptian Religion.

Why are the Gods and Goddesses worshipped?

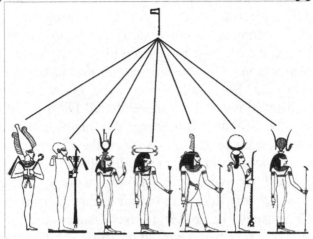

Neter and the Neteru
The Neteru (Gods and Goddesses) proceed
from the Neter (Supreme Being)

As stated earlier, the concept of Neter and Neteru binds and ties all of the varied forms of Kamitan spirituality into one vision of the gods and goddesses all emerging from the same Supreme Being. Therefore, ultimately, Kamitan spirituality is not polytheistic, nor is it monotheistic, for it holds that the Supreme Being is more than a God or Goddess. The Supreme Being is an all-encompassing Absolute Divinity.

"Neteru"

The term "Neteru" means "gods and goddesses." This means that from the ultimate and transcendental Supreme Being, "Neter," come the Neteru. There are countless Neteru. So from the one come the many. These Neteru are cosmic forces that pervade the universe. They are the means by which Neter sustains Creation and manifests through it. So Neterianism is a monotheistic polytheism. The one Supreme Being expresses as many gods and goddesses and at the end of time, after their work of sustaining Creation is finished, these gods and goddesses are again absorbed back into the Supreme Being.

Shetaut Neter religion recognizes that there is one supreme and transcendental Divinity- as in all other African religions. However, this divinity cannot be known by the unenlightened mind. For that reason images that the mind can grasp have been created by the sages of ancient times to allow a person to direct their attention and devotion towards an aspect of the Divine. Since all aspects (the gods and goddesses) are regarded as manifestations of the transcendental Divine Self which has no form or name, the worship (directing the heart and mind) of these divinities gradually leads to the discovery of their transcendental essence. In this manner the worship of any of the divinities (neteru) if entered into correctly, will lead to awakening. So the worship of the gods and goddesses is a proper way to lead the mind to discovery of the perspective of higher consciousness. In order to have success it is necessary to worship in two ways, by ritual, chant and offering to the divinity and next by study of the qualities, myth and teaching of the divinity (Devotion and Wisdom). As a divinity is discovered an aspect of the transcendental divine is discovered and if all divinities are known then the transcendental divine is also known. The teachings of Shetaut Neter are disseminated through the different branches of Shetaut Neter Religion. Each branch constitutes a variation on the original theological teaching of Shetaut Neter religious philosophy through different but related divinities that all ultimately emanate from the single original ONE. Below are the main traditions of Shetaut Neter Ancient Egyptian Religion.

The Anunian Tradition

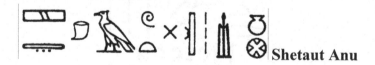 **Shetaut Anu**

The Mystery Teachings of the Anunian Tradition are related to the Divinity Ra and his company of Gods and Goddesses.[1] This Temple and its related Temples espouse the teachings of Creation, human origins and the path to spiritual enlightenment by means of the Supreme Being in the form of the god Ra. It tells of how Ra emerged from a primeval ocean and how human beings were created from his tears. The gods and goddesses, who are his children, go to form the elements of nature and the cosmic forces that maintain nature.

---

[1] See the Book Anunian Theology by Muata Ashby

16

Top: Ra. From top and left to right, The Gods and Goddesses of Anunian Theology: Ra, Shu, Tefnut, Geb, Nut, Aset, Asar, Set, Nebthet and Heru-Ur

The Theban Tradition

 **Shetaut Amun**

The Mystery Teachings of the Wasetian Tradition are related to the Neterus known as Amun, Mut Khonsu. This temple and its related temples espoused the teachings of Creation, human origins and the path to spiritual enlightenment by means of the Supreme Being in the form of the god Amun or Amun-Ra. It tells of how Amun and his family, the Trinity of Amun, Mut and Khonsu, manage the Universe along with his Company of Gods and Goddesses. This Temple became very important in the early part of the New Kingdom Era.

See the Book *Egyptian Yoga Vol. 2* for more on Amun, Mut and Khonsu by Muata Ashby

The Goddess Tradition

Shetaut Netrit

"Arat"

The hieroglyphic sign Arat means "Goddess." General, throughout ancient Kamit, the Mystery Teachings of the Goddess Tradition are related to the Divinity in the form of the Goddess. The Goddess was an integral part of all the Neterian traditions but special temples also developed around the worship of certain particular Goddesses who were also regarded as Supreme Beings in their own right. Thus as in other African religions, the goddess as well as the female gender were respected and elevated as the male divinities. The Goddess was also the author of Creation, giving birth to it as a great Cow. The following are the most important forms of the goddess.[2]

Aset, Net, Sekhmit, Mut, Hetheru

**Mehurt ("The Mighty Full One")**

---

[2] See the Books, *The Goddess Path, Mysteries of Aset, Glorious Light Meditation, Memphite Theology* and *Resurrecting Asar* by Muata Ashby

The Asarian Tradition

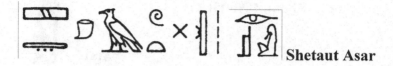 **Shetaut Asar**

This temple and its related temples espoused the teachings of Creation, human origins and the path to spiritual enlightenment by means of the Supreme Being in the form of the god Asar. It tells of how Asar and his family, the Trinity of Asar, Aset and Heru, manage the Universe and lead human beings to spiritual enlightenment and the resurrection of the soul. This Temple and its teaching were very important from the Pre-Dynastic era down to the Christian period. The Mystery Teachings of the Asarian Tradition are related to the Neterus known as: Asar, Aset, Heru (Asar, Aset and Heru)

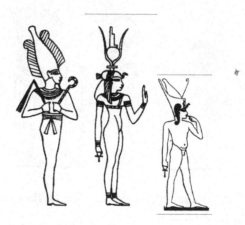

The tradition of Asar, Aset and Heru was practiced generally throughout the land of ancient Kamit. The centers of this tradition were the city of Abdu containing the Great Temple of Asar, the city of Pilak containing the Great Temple of Aset[3] and Edfu containing the Ggreat Temple of Heru.

---

[3] See the Book Resurrecting Asar by Muata Ashby

The Aton Tradition

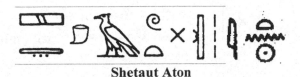

Shetaut Aton

This temple and its related temples espoused the teachings of Creation, human origins and the path to spiritual enlightenment by means of the Supreme Being in the form of the god Aton. It tells of how Aton with its dynamic life force created and sustains Creation. By recognizing Aton as the very substratum of all existence, human beings engage in devotional exercises and rituals and the study of the Hymns containing the wisdom teachings of Aton explaining that Aton manages the Universe and leads human beings to spiritual enlightenment and eternal life for the soul. This Temple and its teaching were very important in the middle New Kingdom Period. The Mystery Teachings of the Aton Tradition are related to the Neter Aton and its main exponent was the Sage King Akhnaton, who is depicted below with his family adoring the sundisk, symbol of the Aton.

Akhnaton, Nefertiti and Daughters

For more on Atonism and the Aton Theology see the Essence of Atonism Lecture Series by Sebai Muata Ashby ©2001

The Memphite Tradition

  **Shetaut Menefer**

Below: The
Memphite
Cosmogony.

The city of Hetkaptah (Ptah)

The Neters of Creation -
The Company of the Gods and Goddesses.
Neter Neteru
Nebertcher - Amun **(unseen, hidden, ever present,
Supreme Being, beyond duality and description)**

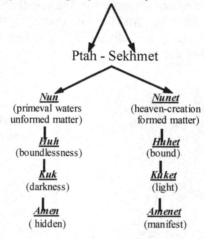

Ptah - Sekhmet

Nun
(primeval waters
unformed matter)

Nunet
(heaven-creation
formed matter)

Huh
(boundlessness)

Huhet
(bound)

Kuk
(darkness)

Kuket
(light)

Amen
(hidden)

Amenet
(manifest)

The Mystery Teachings of the Menefer (Memphite) Tradition are related to the Neterus known as Ptah, Sekhmit, Nefertem. The myths and philosophy of these divinities constitutes Memphite Theology.[4] This temple and its related temples espoused the teachings of Creation, human origins and the path to spiritual enlightenment by means of the Supreme Being in the form of the god Ptah and his family, who compose the Memphite Trinity. It tells of how Ptah emerged from a primeval ocean and how he created the universe by his will and the power of thought (mind). The gods and goddesses who are his thoughts, go to form the elements of nature and the cosmic forces that maintain nature. His spouse, Sekhmit has

---

[4] See the Book Memphite Theology by Muata Ashby

a powerful temple system of her own that is related to the Memphite teaching. The same is true for his son Nefertem.

Ptah, Sekhmit and Nefertem

The Forces of Entropy in Shetaut Neter Religious Traditions

In Neterian religion, there is no concept of "evil" as is conceptualized in Western Culture. Rather, it is understood that the forces of entropy are constantly working in nature to bring that which has been constructed by human hands to their original natural state. The serpent Apep (Apophis), who daily tries to stop Ra's boat of creation, is the symbol of entropy. This concept of entropy has been referred to as "chaos" by Western Egyptologists.

Apep

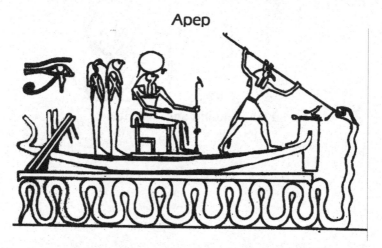

Above: Set protecting the boat of Ra from the forces of entropy (symbolized by the serpent Apep).

Set

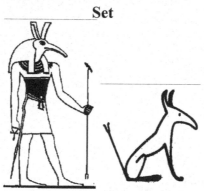

Set and the Set animal

As expressed previously, in Neterian religion there is also no concept of a "devil" or "demon" as is conceived in the Judeo-Christian or Islamic traditions. Rather, it is understood that manifestations of detrimental situations and adversities arise as a result of unrighteous actions. These unrighteous actions are due to the "Setian" qualities in a human being. Set is the Neteru of egoism and the negative qualities which arise from egoism. Egoism is the idea of individuality based on identification with the body and mind only as being who one is. One has no deeper awareness of their deeper spiritual essence, and thus no understanding of their connectedness to all other objects (includes persons) in creation and the Divine Self. When the ego is under the control of the higher nature, it fights the forces of entropy (as above). However, when beset with ignorance, it leads to the degraded states of human existence. The vices (egoism, selfishness, extraverted ness, wonton sexuality (lust), jealousy, envy, greed, gluttony) are a result.

Sacred Scriptures of Shetaut Neter

The following scriptures represent the foundational scriptures of Kamitan culture. They may be divided into three categories: *Mythic Scriptures*, *Mystical Philosophy* and *Ritual Scriptures*, and *Wisdom Scriptures* (Didactic Literature). The Chants, Divine Singing lyrics and recitations contained in this book/manual are all derived from the scriptures below.

MYTHIC SCRIPTURES Literature	Mystical (Ritual) Philosophy Literature	Wisdom Texts Literature
Shetaut Asar-Aset-Heru The Myth of Asar, Aset and Heru (Asarian Resurrection Theology) - Predynastic	Coffin Texts (c. 2040 B.C.E.-1786 B.C.E.) Papyrus Texts (c. 1580 B.C.E.-Roman Period)5 Books of Coming Forth By Day Example of famous papyri: Papyrus of Any Papyrus of Hunefer Papyrus of Kenna Greenfield Papyrus, Etc.	Wisdom Texts (c. 3,000 B.C.E. – Ptolemaic Period) Precepts of Ptahotep Instructions of Any Instructions of Amenemope Etc. Maat Declarations Literature (All Periods) Blind Harpers Songs
Shetaut Atum-Ra Anunian Theology Predynastic		
Shetaut Net/Aset/Hetheru Saitian Theology – Goddess Spirituality Predynastic		
Shetaut Ptah Memphite Theology Predynastic		
Shetaut Amun Theban Theology Predynastic		

---

[5] After 1570 B.C.E they would evolve into a more unified text, the Egyptian Book of the Dead.

Brief Gloss on the Neterian Great Truths

See the Book Principles of Shetaut Neter-African Religion for more details. For the purpose of the practice of the spiritual program, the great truths are to be recited 4 (four) times at the commencement of the daily, monthly or annual spiritual program. Other scriptures may be added to these.

1. "Pa Neter ua ua Neberdjer m Neteru" -"The Neter, the Supreme Being, is One and alone and as Neberdjer, manifesting everywhere and in all things in the form of Gods and Goddesses."

Neberdjer means "all-encompassing divinity," the all-inclusive, all-embracing Spirit which pervades all and who is the ultimate essence of all. This first truth unifies all the expressions of Kamitan religion.

2. "an-Maat swy Saui Set s-Khemn" - "Lack of righteousness brings fetters to the personality and these fetters lead to ignorance of the Divine."

When a human being acts in ways that contradict the natural order of nature, negative qualities of the mind will develop within that person's personality. These are the afflictions of Set. Set is the neteru of egoism and selfishness. The afflictions of Set include: anger, hatred, greed, lust, jealousy, envy, gluttony, dishonesty, hypocrisy, etc. So to be free from the fetters of set one must be free from the afflictions of Set.

3. "s-Uashu s-Nafu n saiu Set" -"Devotion to the Divine leads to freedom from the fetters of Set."

To be liberated (Nafu - freedom - to breath) from the afflictions of Set, one must be devoted to the Divine. Being devoted to the Divine means living by Maat. Maat is a way of life that is purifying to the heart and beneficial for society as it promotes virtue and order. Living by Maat means practicing Shedy (spiritual practices and disciplines).

Uashu means devotion and the classic pose of adoring the Divine is called "Dua," standing or sitting with upraised hands facing outwards towards the image of the divinity.

4. "ari Shedy Rekh ab m Maakheru" - "The practice of the Shedy disciplines leads to knowing oneself and the Divine. This is called being True of Speech."

Doing Shedy means to study profoundly, to penetrate the mysteries (Shetaut) and discover the nature of the Divine. There have been several practices designed by the sages of Ancient Kamit to facilitate the process of self-knowledge. These are the religious (Shetaut) traditions and the Sema (Smai) Tawi (yogic) disciplines related to them that augment the spiritual practices.

All the traditions relate the teachings of the sages by means of myths related to particular gods or goddesses. It is understood that all of these neteru are related, like brothers and sisters, having all emanated from the same source, the same Supremely Divine parent, who is neither male nor female, but encompasses the totality of the two.

Shetaut Neter: The Path of Awakening

What is The Great Awakening?

"Nehast"

Nehast means to "wake up," to Awaken to the higher existence. In the Prt m Hru Text it is said:

Nuk pa Neter aah Neter Uah asha ren[6]

"I am that same God, the Supreme One, who has myriad of mysterious names."

The goal of all the Neterian disciplines is to discover the meaning of "Who am I?," to unravel the mysteries of life and to fathom the depths of eternity and infinity. This is the task of all human beings and it is to be accomplished in this very lifetime.

This can be done by learning the ways of the Neteru, emulating them and finally becoming like them, Akhus, (enlightened beings), walking the earth as giants and accomplishing great deeds such as the creation of the universe!

Udjat

The Eye of Heru is a quintessential symbol of awakening to Divine Consciousness, representing the concept of Nehast.

---

[6] (Prt M Hru 9:4)

What is the purpose of Neterianism? What is the purpose of all the disciplines of Neterian spirituality?

The end of all the Neterian disciplines is to discover the meaning of "Who am I," to unravel the mysteries of life and to fathom the depths of eternity and infinity. This is the task of all human beings and it is to be accomplished in this very lifetime.

This can be done by learning the ways of the Neteru, emulating them and finally becoming like them, Akhus, (enlightened beings), walking the earth as giants and accomplishing great deeds such as the creation of the universe!

The Kemetic word "Nehast" means attaining that sublime and highest goal of life which is Spiritual Enlightenment, to experience the state of conscious awareness of oneness with the Divine and all Creation which transcends individuality born of ego consciousness…like the river uniting with the ocean, discovering the greater essential nature of Self… that state which bestows abiding blessedness, peace, bliss, contentment, fulfillment, freedom from all limitation and supreme empowerment. How is the Highest Goal of Shetaut Neter to be Realized in Life?

What is Sema Tawi?   What is Shedy?

"Sema Tawi (or Smai Tawi)"
(*Egyptian Yoga*)
(From Chapter 4 of the *Prt m Hru*)

"Shedy"

Shedy means: "to penetrate the mysteries", "to study the teachings deeply and gain insight into their meaning."

In Chapter 4 and Chapter 17 of the Prt m Hru, a term "Sma (Sema or Smai) Tawi" is used. It means "Union of the two lands of Egypt," ergo "Egyptian Yoga." The two lands refer to the two main districts of the country (North and South). In ancient times, Egypt was divided into two sections or land areas. These were known as Lower and Upper Egypt. In Ancient Egyptian mystical philosophy, the land of Upper Egypt relates to the divinity Heru (Horus), who represents the Higher Self, and the land of Lower Egypt relates to Set, the divinity of the lower self. So Sema (Smai) Tawi means "the union of the two lands" or the "Union of the lower self with the Higher Self. The lower self relates to that which is negative and uncontrolled in the human mind including worldliness, egoism, ignorance, etc. (Set), while the Higher Self relates to that which is above temptations and is good in the human heart as well as in touch with Transcendental consciousness (Heru). Thus, we also have the Ancient Egyptian term Sema (Smai) Heru-Set, or the union of Heru and Set. So Sema (Smai) Tawi or Sema (Smai) Heru-Set are the Ancient Egyptian words which are to be translated as "Egyptian Yoga."

What Are The Disciplines of Shedy?

There were 4 aspects of Shedy (Spiritual Practice):

1 . *Sedjm - "Listening"*
2 . *Maat - "Right Actions"*
3 . *Uash - "Devotion to God"*
4 . *Uaa - "Meditation"*

Each discipline of Shedy is designed to inform, purify, elevate and establish the Shemsu on the path to awakening. These are the steps to the effective practice of religion that will lead a human being to maturity and spiritual realization.

So it is clear to see that Uash or Ushet is an integral aspect of Shetaut Neter (religion) and the discipline of Shedy as a form of Sema (Yoga) practice. This means that there is no contradiction between the practice of religion and yoga. Rather the sema (yogic) movement should be thought of as a technology to make the religion effective. In fact, from this advanced the practice of religion without the disciplines that purify the heart and lead to a metaphysical realization of higher consciousness cannot be considered as a viable religious system for attaining spiritual awakening. Therefore, the aspirant should practice the disciplines of Devotion no matter what inclination there may be, towards religion or yogic techniques. Both are necessary for ultimate success.

THE PURPOSE OF DIVINE WORSHIP

This manual has been composed with original prayers, words of power and meditations on the Divine from Ancient Egyptian sources. Due to the scope of this volume it would be impossible to explain in detail the mystical teachings contained in each utterance. However, we have attempted to provide a basic knowledge related to the prayers and utterances. It is strongly suggested that you seek further instruction from the Shetaut Neter Book Series. you may send for the Egyptian Yoga Catalog and the Egyptian Yoga Guide. These two free pamphlets provide information about the teachings and the contents of the book series on Ancient Egyptian Yoga and mystical spirituality.

The purpose of Ushet is to engender understanding and closeness with the Divine. So as you study and practice the teachings their deeper subtle and mystical meaning will be revealed to you automatically.

WHAT ARE Uashu and Shedy?

Uashu or Ushet means "to worship the Divine," "to propitiate the Divine." Ushet is of two types, external and internal. When you go to pilgrimage centers, temples, spiritual gatherings, etc., you are practicing external worship or spiritual practice. When you go into your private meditation room on your own and your utter words of power, prayers and meditation you are practicing internal worship or spiritual practice.

Ushet needs to be understood as a process of not only an outer show of spiritual practice, but it is also a process of developing love for the Divine. Therefore, Ushet really signifies a development in Devotion towards the Divine. This practice is also known as sma uash or Yoga of Devotion. Ushet is the process of discovering the Divine and allowing your heart to flow towards the Divine. This program of life allows a spiritual aspirant to develop inner peace, contentment and universal love, and these qualities lead to spiritual enlightenment or union with the Divine. It is recommended that you see the book "The Path of Divine Love" by Dr. Muata Ashby. This volume will give details into this form of Sema or Yoga.

Hekau or "words of power" are utterances which can be used to promote spiritual wisdom, health and well being, mental concentration and the transformation in consciousness. More will be elaborated on hekau in the section on words of power.

Shedy or Sheti: Spiritual discipline or program, to go deeply into the mysteries, to study the mystery teachings and literature profoundly, to penetrate the mysteries. Thus, Sheti signifies "spiritual discipline or program for promoting the understanding of Shetai (Hidden Supreme Being) and growing spiritually in a process leading towards spiritual enlightenment."

"O behold with thine eye God's plans. Devote thyself to adore God's name. It is God who giveth Souls to millions of forms, and God magnifyeth whosoever magnifieth God."

GOD is hidden to Gods and men...GOD's name remains hidden...It is a mystery to his children (men, women, Gods) GOD's names are innumerable, manifold and no one knows their number."

"If you seek GOD, you seek for the Beautiful. One is the Path that leads unto GOD - Devotion joined with Knowledge."

"Seekest thou God, thou seekest for the Beautiful. One is the Path that leadeth unto It - Devotion joined with wisdom."

-Ancient Egyptian-African Proverbs

This teaching means that the path to the Divine is achieved with devotion to the Divine, implying the practice of developing increasing love for the Divine that gradually becomes all-encompassing and enlightening. That devotion is to be expressed in love for all things, primarily, the forms of the Divine that have been handed down by the sages of ancient Kamit. Then to its manifestations in creation. Further, it means the practice of that devotion through disciplines of the devotional path (chant, divine singing, meditation, etc.) including the performance of ritual. Increasing devotion leads to opening of the heart and melting the egoistic aspects of the personality which form the mental obstructions to spiritual realization.

Also the proverb implies that that devotion cannot be based on blind faith and emotionality. Rather, feeling in the practice of religion is to be tempered and augmented with wisdom. Wisdom comes from the study of spiritual texts, reflecting on the exposition of the teaching by qualified sages and then meditating upon that teaching, allowing it and it alone to occupy the mental space so that eventually one becomes one with the knowledge and that knowledge reveals itself as the experience of the innermost Self, the same object of supreme devotion. Then having experienced the knowledge it is realized as wisdom. This is what it means to truly be a shemsu (follower) of the religion.

TWO FORMS OF WORHIP

In ancient times there were two forms of worship. One is the Temple worship which was composed of private worship by the priests and priestesses and public worship led by the priests and priestesses. The other was the private worship in peoples homes. Ordinary people were to set up a temple room in their homes to conduct personal devotional practices.

Personal private altar in home of Egyptian man 18 dynasty

AMULETS AND INVOCATIONS

Amulets and invocatory words of power are used for daily worship with great frequency. One popular amulet is the scarab, the symbol of Khepri the Creator and illuminer of all. Another popular form of amulet is to be carried or worn and is the protective scroll. It is a small roll of papyrus with an invocatory inscription written in hieroglyphic text. It was also often given to children to protect them from negative forces and procure the presence of the Divine in their lives. An example of the scroll is below: a small piece of papyrus with an inscription rolled up and placed in a cylindrical container and warn as a pendant around the neck. Any chant or wisdom teaching will be efficacious for this amulet ritual practice.

Above: Ancient Egyptian protection pendant.
Below: Invocation for the protection of a child.

Words of power for a knot
for a child, a fledgling:

Are you hot in the nest? Are you burning in the bush? Your mother is not with you? There is no sister there to fan you? There is no nurse to offer protection? Let there be brought to me a pellet of gold, 40 bread pellets, a cornelian seal-stone, with a crocodile and hand on it, to fell, to drive off this Demon of Desire, to warm the limbs, to fell these male and female enemies from the West. You shall break out!

This is a protection.

ONE SHALL SAY THIS HEKAU OVER THE PELLET OF GOLD, THE 40 BREAD PELLETS, AND THE CORNELIAN SEAL-STONE, -WITH- THE CROCODILE AND THE HAND.' TO BE STRUNG ON A STRIP OF FINE LINEN; MADE INTO AN AMULET; PLACED ON THE NECK OF THE CHILD, GOOD.

THE PATH OF DIVINE LOVE

Scriptures: Prt M Hru and Temple Inscriptions.

1– Listening to the myth
   Get to know the Divinity
   Empathize
   Romantisize

2-Ritual about the myth
   Offerings to Divinity – propitiation
   act like divinity
   Chant the name of the Divinity
   Sing praises of the Divinity (Divine Singing)
   COMMUNE with the Divinity

3– Mysticism
   Melting of the heart
   Dissolve into Divinity
   IDENTIFY-with the Divinity

Uash Neter or *The Path of Divine Love* is an essential element of Shetaut Neter or Neterianism-Ancient Egyptian (African Religion). The practice of Devotion to the Divine is an integral part of the movement towards spiritual awakening and enlightenment. Devotion to and the repetition of the Divine Name is an integral part of the Path of Divine Love which encompasses the disciplines for promoting spiritual evolution by harnessing the feeling capacity of the human heart. The chanting and praising of the Divine Name is the process of uttering *Hekau* (Words of Power) containing the name of the chosen divinity being worshipped in a format of recitation and rhythmic, repetition called *Hessi*. Divine singing makes use of musical forms to intensify the divine feeling experience.

Music has a profound effect on the unconscious mind. Have you wondered at the fact that you may forget things and events of the past but if you hear a song from that time, the feelings come back. Feeling has more staying power than thoughts but without thought (wisdom) feelings degrade to the level of sentimental blind faith. So music is used to "feel" the teaching and allow It to have a more profound effect on the personality. The disciplines of the Path of Divine Love are designed to purify the heart, allow a human being to come closer to the Divine and eventually become one with the Divine. There are three important stages in the process of cultivating Neter Merri (Divine Love); Listening to the mythic teaching, practicing the ritual of the myth and entering into the metaphysical (mystical) reality of the myth. The practice of daily devotional chant, divine singing, and divine worship are integral, though not confined to the second stage of the Path of Divine Love.

In the Kamitan teaching of Devotional Love:

God is termed *Merri*, "Beloved One"

The aspirant is the Beloved

"That person (the aspirant) is beloved by the Lord."
PMH, Ch 4

PRACTICING Divine Worship

Divine Worship is the process of directing the personality towards the Divine by means of the emotion and feeling capacity of the personality. This means that one's desire, one's caring capacity, one's devotion and one's love are all directed at the Divine. This has the effect of turning the personality towards what is higher that the little self, first of all. Next it has the effect of rendering the ego humble and inconsequential since loving the Divine does not lead to egoistic attachment, but rather universal admiration and reverence. Since there are not personal objects or sentimental worldly relations there can be no fluctuation or loss of the Divine Love as there is in worldly human love. Therefore, a great peace comes over the personality in the practice of Divine Worship since it quickly becomes obvious that the object of the Divine Worship, i.e. God(dess), is always there in the heart, and everywhere else and can never be lost. In this manner, Divine Worship transforms the personality, rendering it humble, peaceful and enlightened.

Tools For Divine Worship

Basic necessities for effective worship: every Shemsu should have the following items available for the daily practice of Shetaut Neter:

In order to enhance your daily spiritual practice you should set up an altar with certain basic materials which will assist you in focusing your mind on your worship disciplines (prayer, chanting, meditation). Set up the altar in the eastern or northern wall of your room so that you can make your sitting posture facing east or north.

Essentials:

☥ Divine image – (on paper or as sculpture (statue)) image of your tutelary divinity
☥ Scroll with four truths and audio cassette meditation chant tape.
☥ Ankh amulet
☥ Candle
☥ Incense
☥ Prayer mat or blanket

tu·te·lar·y (tōōt′l-ĕr′ē, tyōōt′-) also **tu·te·lar** (tōōt′l-ər, -är′, tyōōt′-) - *-adj.* **1.** Being or serving as a guardian or protector. **2.** Of or relating to a guardian or guardianship.

The tutelary divinity is the god or goddess that most appeals to your sensibility. It is the most fascinating and interesting to you and who you feel a connection to. The worship of this divinity (be revering its image and symbolism and studying its mythic teaching), along with the guidance of the spiritual preceptor, will guide you towards spiritual awakening and enlightenment.

Very Important:

♦ Attend Neterian class and spiritual services locally and/or online whenever possible.
♦ Book to read and study independently.
♦ Audio lecture related to the book for greater insight.
♦ Audio recordings of chants and divine singing to chant and sing along with if you are not part of a worship group.

Important:

♦ Attend Neterian seminars and workshops related to the practice and study of Shetaut Neter.
♦ Pilgrimages – make pilgrimages to the original Holy Land of Kamit to experience the power of Shetaut Neter – first hand, if possible with guidance from qualified Neterian teachers.

WORDS OF POWER IN MEDITATION: Khu-Hekau, Mantra Repetition:

In Neterian (Ancient Egyptian religion) terminology, "hekau" or word formulas are recited with meaning and feeling to achieve the desired end of controlling the mind and inculcating it with the vibrations of higher consciousness.

Hekau-mantra recitation or Hesi, (called *Japa* in India), is especially useful in changing the mental state. The sounds coupled with ideas or meditations based on a profound understanding of the meaning can have the effect of calming the mind by directing its energy toward sublime thoughts rather than toward degrading, pain filled ones. This allows the vibrations of the mind to be changed. There are three types of recitations that can be used with the words of power: 1- Mental, 2- Recitation employing a soft humming sound and 3- loud or audible reciting. The main purpose of reciting the words of power is somewhat different than prayer. Prayer involves you as a subject, "talking" to God, while words of power - hekau, are used to carry your consciousness to divine levels by changing the vibrations in your mind and allowing it to transcend the awareness of the senses, body and ordinary thought processes.

The recitation of words of power has been explored to such a degree that it constitutes an important form of yoga practice. Pupils may repeat their hekau as many as 50,000 per day. If this level of practice is maintained, it is possible to achieve specific changes in a short time. Otherwise, changes in your level of mental awareness, self-control, mental peace and spiritual realization occur according to your level of practice. You should not rush nor suppress your spiritual development, rather allow it to gradually grow into a fire which engulfs the mind as your spiritual aspiration grows in a natural way.

Hekau can be directed toward worldly attainments or toward spiritual attainment in the form of enlightenment. There are words of power for gaining wealth or control over others. We will present Egyptian, Indian and Christian words of power which are directed to self-control and mental peace leading to spiritual realization of the Higher Self. You may choose from the list according to your level of understanding and practice.

41

If you were initiated into a particular hekau or mantra by an authentic spiritual preceptor, we recommend that you use that one as your main meditative sound formula. You may use others for singing according to your inclination in your leisure or idle time. Also you may use shortened versions for chanting or singing when not engaged in formal practice. For example, if you choose "Om Amun Ra Ptah", you may also use "Om Amun".

Reciting words of power is like making a well. If a well is made deep enough, it yields water. If the words of power are used long enough and with consistency, they yield spiritual vibrations which reach deep into the unconscious mind to cut through the distracting thoughts and then reveal the deeper you. If they are not used with consistency, they are like shallow puddles which get filled easily by rain, not having had a chance to go deeply enough to reveal what lies within. Don't forget that your movement in yoga should be balanced and integrated. Therefore, continue your practice of the other major disciplines we have described along with your practice of reciting the hekau. Mental recitation is considered to be the most powerful. However, in the beginning you may need to start with recitation aloud until you are able to control the mind's wandering. If it wanders, simply return to the words of power (hekau). Eventually the words of power will develop their own staying power. You will even hear them when you are not consciously reciting. They will begin to replace the negative thought patterns of the mind and lead the mind toward serenity and from here to spiritual realization. When this occurs you should allow yourself to feel the sweetness of reciting the divine names.

As discussed earlier, HEKAU may be used to achieve control over the mind and to develop the latent forces that are within you. Hekau or mantras are mystic formulas which an aspirant uses in a process of self-alchemy. The chosen words of power may be in the form of a letter, word or a combination of words which hold a specific mystical meaning to lead the mind to deeper levels of concentration and to deeper levels of understanding of the teaching behind the words. You may choose one for yourself or you my use one that you were initiated into by a spiritual preceptor. Also, you may have a special hekau for meditation and you may still use other hekau, prayers, hymns or songs of praise according to your devotional feeling. Once you choose a hekau, the practice involves its repetition with meaning and feeling to the point of becoming one with it.

You will experience that the words of power drop from your mind and there are no thoughts but just awareness. This is the soul level where you begin to transcend thoughts and body identification. You may begin practicing it out loud (verbally) and later practice in silence (mentally). At some point your level of concentration will deepen. At that point your mind will disengage from all external exercises and take flight into the unknown, uncharted waters of the subconscious, the unconscious, and beyond. Simply remain as a detached witness and allow yourself to grow in peace. Listed below are several hekau taken from ancient Egyptian texts. They may be used in English or in ancient Kemetic according to your choice.

If you feel a certain affinity toward a particular energy expressed through a particular deity, use that inclination to your advantage by aligning yourself with that energy and then directing it toward the divine within your heart. Never forget that while you are working with a particular deity in the beginning stages, your objective is to delve into the deeper mystical implications of the symbolic form and characteristics of the deity. These always refer to the transcendental Self which is beyond all deities. According to your level of advancement you may construct your own Hekau according to your own feeling and understanding. As a rule, in meditations such as those being discussed now, the shorter the size of the hekau the more effective it will be since you will be able repeat it more often. However, the shorter the hekau, the more concentration it requires so as not to get lost in thoughts. You may wish to begin with a longer hekau and shorten it as your concentration builds. Words of power have no power in and of themselves. It is the user who gives them power through understanding and feeling.

When practicing the devout ritual identification form of meditation, the recitation of hymns, the wearing of costumes and elaborate amulets and other artifacts may be used. Ritual identification with the divine may be practiced by studying and repeatedly reading the various hymns to the divine such as those which have been provided in this volume, while gradually absorbing and becoming one with the teachings as they relate to you. When a creation hymn is being studied, you should reflect upon it as your true Self being the Creator, as your true Self being the hero(heroine), and that you (your true essence) are the one being spoken about in all the teachings. It is all about you. "You" are the Creator. "You" are the sustainer of the universe. "You" are the only one who can achieve transcendence through enlightenment according to your own will. When you feel, think and act this way, you are using the highest form of worship and meditation toward the divine by constantly bringing the mind back to the idea that all is the Self and that you essentially are that Self. This form of practice is higher than any ritual or any other kind of offering. Here you are concentrating on the idea that your limited personality is only an expression of the divine. You are laying down your ego on the offering mat.

The following outline for the frequency of possible recitations is provided as a guideline. We have included two types of words of power: short, containing one or two syllables, medium length, containing two to three and average, containing six to eight. They are presented as guidelines for practice of hekau-mantra repetition practice.

Generally, when the words of power are used over a sustained period of time, the benefits or psychic powers arise. The most important psychic powers you can attain to facilitate your spiritual program are peace, serenity of mind, and concentration of the mental vibrations. Concentration opens the door to transcendental awareness and spiritual realization. Various estimates are given as to when you may expect to feel results; these vary from 500,000 repetitions to 1,200,000 or more. The number should not be your focus. Sustained practice, understanding the teachings about the Self and practicing of the virtues and self-control in an integral, balanced fashion are the most important factors determining your eventual success.

While *Om* is most commonly known as a *Sanskrit* mantra (word of power from India), it also appears in the ancient Egyptian texts and is closely related to the Kemetic *Amun*. More importantly, it has the same meaning as Amun and is therefore completely compatible with the energy pattern of the entire group. According to the Egyptian Leyden papyrus, the name of the "Hidden God", referring to Amun, may be pronounced as *Om*, or *Am*.

Om is a powerful sound; it represents the primordial sound of creation. Thus it appears in ancient Egypt as Om, in modern day India as Om, and in Christianity as Amen, being derived from Amun. Om may also be used for engendering mental calm prior to beginning recitation of a longer set of words of power or it may be used alone as described above. One Indian Tantric scripture (*Tattva Prakash*) states that Om or AUM can be used to achieve the mental state free of physical identification and can bring union with *Brahman* (the Absolute transcendental Supreme Being - God) if it is repeated 300,000 times. In this sense, mantras such as Om, Soham, Sivoham, Aham Brahmasmi are called *Moksha Mantras* or mantras which lead to union with the Absolute Self. Their shortness promotes greater concentration and force toward the primordial level of consciousness.

There is one more important divine name which is common to both Indian as well as ancient Egyptian mystical philosophy. The sanskrit mantra ***Hari* Om*** is composed of Om preceded by the word Hari. In Hinduism, *Hari* means: "He who is Tawny". The definition of tawny is: "A light golden brown". This is a reference to the dark colored skin of Vishnu and Krishna. Vishnu is usually depicted with a deep blue and Krishna is depicted with a deep blue or black hue symbolizing infinity and transcendence. Hari is one of Krishna's or Vishnu's many divine names. It also means "hail" as in "hail to the great one" or it may be used as "The Great One". In the ancient Egyptian magical texts used to promote spiritual development (words of power or HEKA - mantras) the word Haari also appears as one of the divine names. Thus, the hekau-mantra Hari Om was also known and used in ancient Egypt and constitutes a most powerful formula for mystical spiritual practice. *(the spelling may be Hari or Hare)

Simply choose a hekau which you feel comfortable with and sit quietly to recite it continuously for a set amount of time. Allow it to gradually become part of your free time when you are not concentrating on anything specific or when you are being distracted by worldly thoughts. This will serve to counteract the worldly or subconscious vibrations that may emerge from the your own unconscious mind. When you feel anger or other negative qualities, recite the hekau and visualize its energy and the deity associated with it destroying the negativity within you.

For example, you may choose ***Amun-Ra-Ptah.*** When you repeat this hekau, you are automatically including the entire system of all gods and goddesses. Amun-Ra-Ptah is known as *Nebertcher,* the "All-encompassing

Divinity". You may begin by uttering it aloud. When you become more advanced in controlling your mind, you may begin to use shorter words. For example simply utter: *Amun, Amun, Amun...* always striving to get to the source of the sound. Eventually you will utter these silently and this practice will carry your consciousness to the source of the sound itself where the very mental instruction to utter is given. Hekau are also related to the spiritual energy centers of the subtle spiritual body (Uraeus-Kundalini).

The following ancient Egyptian selections come from the *"Book of Coming Forth by Day"* and other ancient Egyptian scriptures:

Nuk pu NETER
I am the Supreme Divinity.

Nuk pu Ast
I am ISIS

nuk neter aa kheper tchesef
I am the great God, self created,

Ba ar pet sat ar ta.
Soul is of heaven, body belongs to the earth.

Nuk uab-k uab ka-k uab ba-k uab sekhem.
My mind has pure thoughts, so my soul and life forces are pure.

Nuk ast au neheh ertai-nef tetta.
Behold I am the heir of eternity, everlastingness has been given to me.

Sekhem - a em mu ma aua Set.
I have gained power in the water as I conquered Set (greed, lust, ignorance).

Rex - a em Ab - a sekhem - a em hati - a.
I know my heart, I have gained power over my heart.

Un - na uat neb am pet am ta.
The power is within me to open all doors in heaven and earth.

SEE CHANTING CHART

SCHEDULE FOR DIVINE WORSHIP

"Ra neb Aru"

(DAILY RITUAL)

Daily Shedy -Threefold daily worship – Basic Discipline for the morning.

1 Bathe or Wash face and hands
2 Light candle
3 Light incense
4 Worship- Divine Song
5 Sema Yoga Postures
6 Reciting of the Great Truths
7 Chant – words of scripture
8 Meditation
9 Offering

Worship Ritual – Noon and Dusk
1 Reciting of the Great Truths
2 Divine Chant
3 Meditation

"Abd neb Aru"

(MONTHLY RITUAL)

The Monthly Observances Shetaut Neter

Monthly Observances - Twice monthly moon festival

In addition to the daily worship program:

Festival days

New Moon Fasting 1 day
Full Moon Fasting 1 day

"Renput Aru"

(ANNUAL RITUAL)

The Main Annual Observances of Shetaut Neter

Festival days

Api
Summer Solstice

Nun
Winter Solstice

Annual Schedule for Worship Schedule for Shedy Practice

Sunrise and Sunset Schedule for your Anu, Kamit: is available from The Sema Institute at Semayoga@aol.com upon request for the annual solstice (summer and winter) practice of the global worship. All aspirants around the world synchronize their time and join together at dawn in Egypt for a communal practice of the worship program.

The Daily Worship Schedule for Shedy Practice

Sunrise and Sunset Schedule for your city: is available from www.sunrisesunset.com.

A practitioner of Sema (Yoga) must make an effort to integrate the main practices of yoga into daily life. This means that you need to begin adding small amounts of time for Prayer, Repetition of the Divine Name

(Hekau), Exercise (includes proper breathing exercise), Study of the Teachings, Silence, Selfless Service, Meditation, and Daily Reflection. This also means that you will gradually reduce the practices which go against yogic movement as you gain more time for Sheti.

Below you will find an outline of a schedule for the beginning practice of Yoga. The times given here are a suggested minimum time for beginners. You may spend more time according to your capacity and personal situation, however, try to be consistent in the amount of time and location you choose to practice your discipline as well as in the time of day you choose to perform each of the different practices. This will enable your body and mind to develop a rhythm which will develop into the driving force of your day. When this occurs you will develop stamina and fortitude when dealing with any situation of life. You will have a stable center which will anchor you to a higher purpose in life whether you are experiencing prosperous times or adverse times. In the advanced stages, spiritual practice will become continuous. Try to do the best you can according to your capacity, meaning your circumstances. If your family members are not interested or do not understand what you are trying to do simply maintain your practices privately and try to keep the interruptions to a minimum. As you develop, you may feel drawn toward some forms of practice over others. The important thing to remember is to practice them all in an integrated fashion. Do not neglect any of the practices even though you may spend additional time on some versus others.

Practicing spirituality only during times of adversity is the mistake of those who are spiritually immature. Any form of spiritual practice, ritualistic or otherwise is a positive development, however, you will not derive the optimal spiritual benefits by simply becoming religious when you are in trouble. The masses of people only pray when they are in trouble...then they ask for assistance to get out of trouble. What they do not realize is that if they were to turn their minds to God at all times, not just in times of misfortune, adversity would not befall them. As you progress through your studies you will learn that adversities in life are meant to turn you toward the Divine. In this sense they are messages from the Divine to awaken spiritual aspiration. However, if you do not listen to the message and hearken to the Divine intent behind it, you will be in a position to experience more miseries of life and miseries of a more intense nature.

NOTE 1: The ritual is an important aspect of divine worship- it acts as a metaphysical conduit through which the stream of mental thought will fertilize and germinate the seed of Divine Love that is in the heart. Also, it acts to draw certain cosmic energies (Sekhem) that will be needed to make the spiritual program successful. These energies will be used in bolstering the will and resisting the *inj-set* or fetters of the ego or lower mind. They will be collected and purified and harnessed into a powerful force that will be used to focus the mind and forge your evolved personality through the practice of meditation. The ritual mirrors the divine act of God(dess) daily, who rises with light and warmth in order to care for all- to love all by providing sustenance and the capacity to discover all is one. Therefore it is said that God(dess) is Love, for caring is love. Therefore, an aspirant should learn to love all as an expression of God(dess) and there is no greater way to express love than through caring for all and seeing all as an expression of the Divine. All this and more is contained in the ritual and there are higher expressions (formats) of this ritual for the higher orders of clergy.

NOTE 2: In Neterian culture the morning worship program is regarded as the most important. Therefore, if it is not possible to enjoin the three-fold worship format the morning program can sustain a successful spiritual practice. The traditional time of the morning worship program is at dawn. For the purpose of personal practice the local time may be used. For the purpose of communal practice the worship timing should be attuned to the time of the rising of the sun in the eastern horizon of Kamit in Africa.

NOTE 3: For pronunciations of most of the chants go to www.Egyptianyoga.com or obtain the morning worship recording from the Sema Institute.

Basic Daily Practice of Divine Worship (Uash) and Spiritual Disciplines (outline)

<u>(Make prostration before the altar and the Divine in the east. Assume sitting posture facing the sun)</u>

Ritual step 1 Opening   *your morning worship by uncovering your altar.

Ritual step 2 Lighting Candle   *(Symbolizes the Akhu or Divine Light within that is to be awakened)

Ritual step 3 Lighting Incense   *(Symbolizes the fragrance of your personality which will exude with a divine odor that will rise up and attract as well as commune with the divine)

Ritual step 4 Libation   *Pour purified water from a container on to another receptacle. Pour continuously-silent

Ritual step 5 Offering   *Place offering (live food item-fruit or vegetable) in front of the altar. Also, a figure of Maat may be offered. Recitation of the *OFFERING FORMULA* IS ESSENTIAL. This is what starts the process of divine worship and enables the reciprocation of the divine. During the day, offer your righteousness at your work and in dealing with others, helping the needy- to the Divine

Recitation   *Great Truths (5 minutes)
                **Daily recitations

Chanting   5* minutes using chant book or may use the morning worship tape

51

Divine Singing   5*-10**- Chant *one song
                          minutes using chant book or may use the
                          music CDs to sing along
                          **Select other songs if time
                          allows.

Listening to the philosophy 5*-15** minutes to ½ hour - *Read an
                          Ancient Egyptian Proverb or **Follow
                          along with the ongoing weekly class
                          recordings from the various lecture series.
                          Or may read from scripture or book with
                          teachings explained.

Reflection on the Philosophy   *Silently reflect on the proverb for 5
                          minutes. **Or if more time is available-
                          Keep a Spiritual Journal for writing: Answer
                          the following questions (see below).

Meditation   5* minutes to 30* minutes – follow
                          instructions for the GLM (Ra-Akhu,
                          Glorious Light Meditation system) or may
                          use the meditation tapes or – may use the
                          morning worship tape

Closing invocation   *Chant Om Htp

DAILY WORSHIP PROGRAM INSTRUCTIONS AND TIME FOR THE DAILY WORSHIP DISCIPLINE

*Short program - 30 minutes
**Long program - 45-60 minutes

The program can take between 30 minutes to 1 hour depending on which aspects of the program are enjoined. The abbreviated program is a shortened version of the discipline for those times when the shorter time is available. The asterisks above will clarify which elements are for the shortened* practice and which are for the extended** practice.

The suggested times given above are the minimum amount you should spend on daily spiritual practices each day. Whenever possible you should increase the times according to your capacity and ability. You should train your mind so that it rejoices in hearing about and practicing the teachings of yoga instead of the useless worldly activities. Follow this path gradually but steadily.

Once you have established a schedule of minimal time to devote to practices, even if you do 5-10 minutes of meditation time per day and nothing else, keep your schedule if at all possible. Many people feel that they do not have the time to incorporate even ordinary activities into their lives. They feel overwhelmed with life and feel they have no control. If there is no control it is because there is no discipline. If you make a schedule for all of your activities (spiritual and non-spiritual) and keep to it tenaciously, you will discover that you can control your time and your life. As you discover the glory of spiritual practice, you will find even more time to expand your spiritual program. Ultimately, you will create a lifestyle which is entirely spiritualized. This means that every act in your life will be based on the wisdom teachings (MAAT) and therefore you will not only spend a particular time of day devoted to spiritual practices, but every facet of your life will become a spontaneous worship of the divine.

Questions for discussion after listening to the tapes and readings from the books- answer these in your journal (if you are working independently) discuss with your study group.

       A- What was the message you got from this days lecture?

       B- What insight have you gained into your understanding of spirituality?

       C- How has this teaching affected you today?

       D- How have previous lessons affected your life?

       E- Describe how this lesson or any previous lesson has changed your life from your previous ways into living more in harmony with yourself, nature, humanity or God.

F- How has this or any other lesson from the series given you deeper insight into the previous religion you may have practiced?

THE DAILY WORSHIP PROGRAM INSTRUCTIONS

(Make prostration before the altar and the Divine in the east. Assume
seated posture facing the east or the sun (noon and dusk worship-west)

1.   Ritual step 1 Opening your morning worship by uncovering your
altar.

2.   Ritual step 2 Lighting Candle   (Symbolizes the Akhu or Divine
Light within that is to be awakened)

3.   Ritual step 3 Lighting Incense (Symbolizes the fragrance of your
personality which will exude with a divine odor that will rise up and
attract as well as commune with the divine)

4.   Ritual step 4 Libation -Pour purified water from a container on to
another receptacle. Pour continuously-silent

5.   Offering   Place offering (live food item (fruit or vegetable) in
front of the altar. Recite the Offering Formula FOUR times.

*Hotep di nesu Neter aah Anpu Wep wat neb ta djser per kheru cha Ka-
Aped si Ntr ari Maa-Kheru*

*"Offering is given to the Supreme Divinity and to Anpu and Wepwat, lord
of the sacred land, the spoken offering is 1000 beef (maleness) and 1000
geese (femaleness). This causes the Divine to make one True of Speech."*

6.   ***Recitations for short program-*** Great Truths of Shetaut Neter
(Recite 4 times) for Morning, Noontime and Evening Worship

6b.   ***Additional recitations for long program.*** According to your
time available If more time is available recite one or all of the
prescribed readings for morning, noontime or evening worship

The Divine Offering

Hotep di nesu Neter aah Anpu Wep wat neb ta djser per kheru cha cha-aped si Ntr ari Maa-Kheru

"Offering is given to the Supreme Divinity and to Anpu (preparer of the traveler) and Wepwat (opener of the ways), lord of the sacred land the spoken offering is 1000 beef (complete maleness) and 1000 geese (complete femaleness). This causes the Divine to make one True of Speech (i. e. an enlightened being.)"

Recitations (Readings) for Ushet In The Morning

Opening Prayer A-from the Ancient Egyptian Book of Coming Forth By Day

Dua Ra Cheft Uben F em aket abdet ent Pet
Adorations to Ra When he rises in horizon eastern
Anetej Ra-k iti em Khepera
Homage to Ra, coming forth as Khepera
Khepera qemam neteru
Khepera, Creator of the gods and goddesses
Cha – k uben – k pesd Mut – k
Rising thee, shinning thee, lighting up thy mother
Cha ti em suten neteru
 Rising as Lord, king of the gods and goddesses
Iri – nek mut Nut aiui – em iri nini
Your mother Nut does an act of worship to you with both arms
Manu em hetep hept-tu Maat er tra
Manu (Western Horizon) receives thee in peace, Maat embraces thee at the double season (perennially)

Adorations to Ra when He rises in the Eastern Horizon of Heaven
(From the Hymn to Ra #1 in the Pert m Hru)

Instruction: write your first name in the spaces below and recite your own name as you read.

1. Behold Asar_____ bringing divine offerings of all the gods and goddesses. Asar _____ speaks thus:

2. Homage to thee, who comes in the form of Khepri[7], Khepri the Creator of the gods and goddesses. You rise and shine, illuminating your mother, goddess Nut, the sky, crowned as king of the gods and goddesses. Your mother Nut worships you with her two arms. The western horizon receives you in peace and Maat embraces you at the double season. Give Asar _____ Glorious Spirit being[8], and spiritual strength through righteous speaking. Grant the ability to come forth as a living soul so that

---

[7] Morning sun, solar child-Nefertem.
[8] i.e. allow the initiate to become an Akhu or Glorious Spirit.

Asar _____ may see Heru of the two Horizons.[9] Grant this to the Ka[10] of Asar _____ who is Righteous of Speech in the presence of Asar, the Divine Self. Asar _____ says: Hail to all the gods and goddesses, weighers of the house of the soul, in heaven and on earth by means of the scales of Maat, who are givers of Life Force sustenance.

3. Tatunen,[11] One, maker of men and women as well as the company of the gods and goddesses of the south, the north, the west and the east, i.e. all the neteru[12], grant praises to Ra, the lord of heaven, sovereign of life, vitality and health, maker of the gods and goddesses. Adorations to thee in your form as all goodness, as you rise in your boat. The beings up high praise thee. Beings in the lower realms praise thee. Djehuti[13] and Maat[14] have written for thee, who are shining forth, every day. Your enemies are put to the fire. The fiends are put down, their arms and legs being bound securely for Ra. The children of weakness disrespect and insurrection shall not continue.

4. The great house[15] is in festival time. The voices of the participants are in the great temple. The gods and goddesses are rejoicing. They see Ra in his glorious rising, his beams of light piercing, inundating the lands. This exalted and venerable god journeys on and unites with the land of Manu, the western horizon, illuminating the land of his birth every day and at the same time he reaches the province where he was yesterday.

5. Be in peace with me! I see your beauties and I prosper upon the land; I smile and I defeat the ass fiend as well as the other fiends. Grant that I may defeat Apep[16] in his time of strength and to see the pilot fish of the Divine Boat of Ra, which is in its blessed pool.[17] I see Heru in the form as

---

[9] The All-Encompassing Divine Self in the form of Heru.
[10] Spiritual essence of the personality which holds a person's desires, impulses and impetus to incarnate; the Life Force which sustains the physical being.
[11] Creator -aspect of Ra, Atum, Asar, Khepri, Amun, Neberdjer, etc) who first arose on the primeval mound. Protector of the souls of Asar and Heru.
[12] Gods and goddesses
[13] Ibis headed deity, minister of Ra, originator of hieroglyphic writings and music.
[14] Goddess of righteousness, truth, regularity, and order.
[15] Royal family.
[16] Leader of the fiends, second only to Set.
[17] The pool or lake is the symbol of the Primeval Ocean. In ancient times the temple complexes included a lake for ritually sailing the boat of Ra as well as for keeping fish, crocodiles and other animals as temple mascots.

the guardian of the rudder. Djehuti and Maat are upon his two arms. Received am I in the prow[18] of the Mandet[19] Boat and in the stern of the Mesektet[20] Boat. Ra gives divine sight, to see the Aten[21], to view the moon god unceasingly, every day, and the ability of souls to come forth, to walk to every place they may desire. Proclaim my name! Find him in the wood board of offerings. There have been given to me offerings in the life-giving presence, like it is given to the followers of Heru[22]. It is done for me in the divine place in the boat on the day of the sailing, the journey of The God. I am received in the presence of Asar in the land of truth speaking[23] of the Ka of Asar _____.

*******PAUSE 1 Minute for Silent Meditation*******

Play sistrum in pattern of three shakes three times (123-123-123) then continue

Adorations to Ra-Herakhuti
(From the Hymn to Hymn to Ated by Akhenaten)

Dua Ankh Herakhuti Ha m Akhet
Adorations to the living Horus in the two horizons, residing in the horizon
M ren-f m Shu m Aten
In his name of Shu in the form of the Sundisk
Di ankh djeta heh
Giving life forever and for eternity
In suten ankh m Maat Neb Tawi
This praise is sung by the king (Akhenaten), the living, in righteousness, Lord of the two lands (Ancient Egypt)
Nefer Kheperu Ra ua n Ra
The good king in is name Creator, one with God

---

[18] Front section of a ship's hull, the bow.
[19] The name of Ra's Divine boat when it is traveling from noon to midnight, i.e. the evening boat.
[20] The name of Ra's Divine boat when it is traveling from midnight to noon, i.e. the morning boat.
[21] The sundisk.
[22] In Kemetic Mystical Philosophy the principle of "Shemsu Heru" is very important. It may be likened to the disciples of Jesus in Christianity who were his "followers." It means living and acting like Heru, a life of truth and increasing spiritual enlightenment.
[23] Maak-heru.

Next invoke the assistance of the deity or cosmic force which removes obstacles to your success in spiritual practice. Anpu is the deity which leads souls through the narrow pathways of the Duat. Therefore, request the assistance of Anpu, who represents the discriminative intellectual ability so that you may *"distinguish the real from the unreal"*.

> *"O Apuat* (Anpu), *opener of the ways, the roads of the North, O Anpu, opener of the ways, the roads of the South. The messenger between heaven and hell displaying alternately a face black as night, and golden as the day. He is equally watchful by day as by night."*

> *"May Anpu make my thighs firm so that I may stand upon them".*

> *"I have washed myself in the water wherein the god Anpu washed when he performed the office of embalmer and bandager.*
> *My lips are the lips of Anpu".*

*******PAUSE 1 Minute for Silent Meditation*******

Play sistrum in pattern of three shakes three times (123-123-123) then continue

Next invoke the presence of Aset-Maat who is the embodiment of wisdom and inner discovery of the Divine. Aset (Isis) is the mother of the universe and she herself veils her true form, as the Supreme Transcendental Self. This "veil" of ignorance is only due to ignorance. Therefore, pray for Aset to make her presence, which bestows instant revelation of her true form. This "unveiling" is a metaphor symbolizing the intuitional revelation of the Divine or Enlightenment in your mind. Aset is in your heart and only needs to be revealed. However, she can only reveal herself to the true aspirant, one who is devoted to her (the Self) and her alone. Aset says: *"I Aset, am all that has been, all that is, or shall be; and no mortal man hath ever unveiled me."*

The invocatory prayer to Aset is:

"Oh benevolent Aset, who protected her brother Asar, who searched for him without wearying, who traversed the land in mourning and never rested until she had found him. She who afforded him shadow with her wings and gave him air with her feathers, who rejoiced and carried her brother home.

She who revived what was faint for the weary one, who received his seed and conceived an heir, and who nourished him in solitude while no one knew where he was. . . . "

SPEECH OF ASET. Aset saith:- *I have come to be a protector unto thee. I waft unto thee air for thy nostrils, and the north wind which cometh forth from the god Tem unto thy nose. I have made whole for thee thy windpipe. I make thee to live like a god. Thine enemies have fallen under thy feet. I have made thy word to be true before Nut, and thou art mighty before the gods.*

*******PAUSE 1 Minute for Silent Meditation*******

Play sistrum in pattern of three shakes three times (123-123-123) then continue

Then remember your Spiritual Preceptor, the person who taught you how to meditate, thank them for their teaching and invoke their grace for success in your meditation. *"Have faith in your master's ability to lead you along the path of truth".*

"The lips of the wise are as the doors of a cabinet; no sooner are they opened, but treasures are poured out before you. Like unto trees of gold arranged in beds of silver, are wise sentences uttered in due season."

Now resolve within yourself that you will stay for the prescribed period of time which you have determined and then proceed with the practice as described below. Remember the following precepts: *"Have devotion of purpose", "Have faith in your own ability to accept the truth", "Have faith in your ability to act with wisdom."*

Excerpts of Chapter 33[1] of the Pert M Heru From contemporary papyri[2]

1. I have lived by righteousness and truth while on earth. I live in righteousness a
   truth; I feed upon right and truth in my heart. I have done what is required to live
   harmony in society and the gods and goddesses are also satisfied that I ha
   worshipped rightly.
2. I have done God's will. I have given bread to the hungry, water to the thirsty, cloth
   to the clotheless and a boat to those who were shipwrecked. I made the prescrib
   offerings to the gods and goddesses and I also made offerings in the temple to t
   glorious spirits.
1. Therefore, protect me when I go to face The God.[3]

Closing Devotional Prayer of Aspirants:

amma su en pa neter, sauu – k su emment

en pa neter

au tuanu ma qeti pa haru

"Give thyself to GOD, keep thou thyself daily for God;

and let tomorrow be as today."

Recitations (Readings) for Ushet At Noontime

Opening Prayer A-from the Ancient Egyptian Hymns of Amun*:

O Åmun, O Åmun, who art in heaven, turn thy face upon the dead body of the child, and make your child sound and strong in the Underworld.

O Åmun, O Åmun, O God, O God, O Åmun, I adore thy name, grant thou to me that I may understand thee; Grant thou that I may have peace in the Duat, and that I may possess all my members therein...

Hail, Åmun, let me make supplication unto thee, for I know thy name, and thy transformations are in my mouth, and thy skin is before my eyes. Come, I pray thee, and place thou thine heir and thine image, myself, in the everlasting underworld... let my whole body become like that of a neter, let me escape from the evil chamber and let me not be imprisoned therein; for I worship thy name..

*See the book *Egyptian Yoga Vol 3 Theban Theology* by Dr. Muata Ashby

Visualize that with each utterance you are being enfolded in Divine Grace and Enlightenment.

*******PAUSE 1 Minute for Silent Meditation*******

Play sistrum in pattern of three shakes three times (123-123-123) then continue

Affirmations of Innocence: The 42 Precepts of Maat from the Pert m Heru texts[4]

(1) "I have not done what is wrong." Variant: I have not acted with falsehood.
(2) "I have not robbed with violence."
(3) "I have not done violence (to anyone or anything)." Variant: I have not been rapacious (taking by force; plundering.)
(4) "I have not committed theft." Variant: I have not coveted.
(5) "I have not murdered man or woman." Variant: I have not ordered someone else to commit murder.

63

(6) "I have not defrauded offerings." Variant: <u>I have not destroyed foc</u> <u>supplies or increased or decreased the measures to profit.</u>

(7) "I have not acted deceitfully." Variant: <u>I have not acted with crookedness</u>

(8) "I have not robbed the things that belong to God."

(9) "I have told no lies."

(10) "I have not snatched away food."

(11) "I have not uttered evil words." Variant: <u>I have not allowed myself</u> <u>become sullen, to sulk or become depressed.</u>

(12) "I have attacked no one."

(13) "I have not slaughtered the cattle that are set apart for the Gods." Variar <u>I have not slaughtered the Sacred bull – (Apis)</u>

(14) "I have not eaten my heart" (overcome with anguish and distraugh Variant: <u>I have not committed perjury.</u>

(15) "I have not laid waste the ploughed lands."

(16) "I have not been an eavesdropper or pried into matters to make mischief

(17) "I have not spoken against anyone." Variant: <u>I have not babble</u> <u>gossiped.</u>

(18) "I have not allowed myself to become angry without cause."

(19) "I have not committed adultery." Variant: <u>I have not committe</u> <u>homosexuality.</u>

(20) "I have not committed any sin against my own purity."

(21) "I have not violated sacred times and seasons."

(22) "I have not done that which is abominable."

(23) "I have not uttered fiery words. I have not been a man or woman anger."

(24) "I have not stopped my ears listening to the words of right and wror (Maat)."

(25) "I have not stirred up strife (disturbance)." "I have not caused terror." have not struck fear into any man."

(26) "I have not caused any one to weep." Variant: <u>I have not hoodwinked.</u>

(27) "I have not lusted or committed fornication nor have I lain with others my same sex." Variant: <u>I have not molested children.</u>

(28) "I have not avenged myself." Variant: <u>I have not cultivated resentment.</u>

(29) "I have not worked grief, I have not abused anyone." Variant: <u>I have n</u> <u>cultivated a quarrelsome nature.</u>

(30) "I have not acted insolently or with violence."

(31) "I have not judged hastily." Variant: <u>I have not been impatient.</u>

(32) "I have not transgressed or angered God."

(33) "I have not multiplied my speech overmuch (talk too much).

(34) "I have not done harm or evil." Variant: <u>I have not thought evil.</u>

(35) "I have not worked treason or curses on the King."

(36) "I have never befouled the water." Variant: <u>I have not held back the water from flowing in its season.</u>

(37) "I have not spoken scornfully." Variant: <u>I have not yelled unnecessarily or raised my voice.</u>

(38) "I have not cursed The God."

(39) "I have not behaved with arrogance." Variant: <u>I have not been boastful.</u>[5]

(40) "I have not been overwhelmingly proud or sought for distinctions for myself."[6]

(41) "I have never magnified my condition beyond what was fitting or increased my wealth, except with such things as are (justly) mine own possessions by means of Maat." Variant: <u>I have not disputed over possessions except when they concern my own rightful possessions.</u> Variant: <u>I have not desired more than what is rightfully mine.</u>

(42) "I have never thought evil (blasphemed) or slighted The God in my native town."

Conclusion

I am pure. I am pure. I am Pure.
I have washed my front parts with the waters of libations,
I have cleansed my hinder parts with drugs which make wholly clean, and
my inward parts have been washed in the liquor of Maat

Closing Devotional Prayer of Aspirants:

amma su en pa neter
sauu – k su emment en pa neter
au tuanu ma qeti pa haru

"Give thyself to GOD,
keep thou thyself daily for God;
and let tomorrow be as today."

Recitations (Readings) for Ushet at Sunset

The following is a Hymn to the Supreme Being in the form of Tem or the setting sun. In the theology surrounding the god Ra, Ra is seen as a representation of the Supreme Being (Neberdjer, Pa Neter). As such Ra is depicted as the sun and the sun has three phases which it manifests every day. These phases are the morning, the middle of the day and the setting sun. Thus we have the following quotation:

In the Myth of Ra and Aset Ra says, "I am Khepera in the morning, and Ra at noonday, and Temu in the evening.

Thus, the following hymn is effective for the evening hours, prior to practicing intense meditation and also at the time of death. In the mystical mythology of the ancient Egyptian city of Anu (Sun city) it is understood that Ra travels in barque which is itself the sun. From this barque hang cords by which those who are righteous can grab hold of in order to be lifted unto the boat. Thus through the practice of Maat (righteous living) one is able to be raised to the company of Ra who travels on the boat of millions of years (eternity) and thus attain immortality and communion with God. For more on this teaching see the books Anunian Theology, *Resurrecting Osiris*.

A HYMN TO RA-TEM
(From the papyrus of Lady Mut Hetep)

The lady Mut-Hetep says, "0 Ra-Tem, in thy splendid progress thou risest, and thou settest as a living being "in the glories of the western horizon; thou settest in thy "territory which is in the Mount of Sunset (Manu). "Thy Uraeus is behind thee, thy Uraeus is behind thee. Homage (Ushet) to thee, 0 thou -who art in peace; homage to thee, 0 thou who art in peace. Thou art joined unto the Eye of Tem, and it chooseth its powers of protection [to place] behind thy members. Thou goest forth through heaven, thou travellest over the earth, and thou journeyest onward. 0 Luminary, the northern and southern halves of heaven come to thee, and they bow low in adoration, and they do homage unto thee, day by day. The gods of Amentet rejoice in thy beauties, and the unseen places sing hymns of praise unto thee. Those who dwell in the Sektet boat go round about thee, and the Souls of the East do homage "to thee, and when they meet thy Majesty they cry: "Come, come in peace!" There is a shout of welcome to thee, 0 lord of heaven and governor of Amentet! Thou art acknowledged by Aset (Isis) who seeth her son ,Heru (Horus) in thee, the lord of fear, the mighty one of terror. Thou settest as a living being in the hidden place. Thy father [Ta-]tunen raseth thee up and he placeth both his hands behind thee; thou becomest endowed with divine attributes in [thy] members of earth; thou wakest in peace and thou settest in Manu. Grant thou that I may become a being honoured before Asar (Osiris), and that I may come to thee, 0 Ra-Tem! I have adored thee, therefore do thou for me that which I wish. Grant thou that I may be victorious in the presence of the company of the gods. Thou art beautiful, 0 Ra, in thy western horizon of Amentet, thou lord of Maat, thou being who art greatly feared, and whose attributes are majestic, 0 thou who art greatly beloved by those who dwell in the Duat! Thou shinest with thy beams upon the beings that are therein perpetually, and thou sendest forth thy light upon the path of Ra-stau. Thou openest up the path of the double Lion-god (Aker), thou settest the gods upon [their] thrones, and the spirits in their abiding places. The heart of Naarerf (i.e., An-rut-f, a region of the Underworld) is glad [when] Ra setteth; the heart of Nahrerf is glad when Ra setteth. Hail, 0 ye gods of the land of Amentet who make offerings and oblations unto Ra-Tem, ascribe ye glory [unto him when] ye meet him. Grasp ye your weapons and overthrow ye the fiend Seba on behalf of Ra, and repulse the fiend Nebt on behalf of Asar. The gods of the land of Amentet rejoice and lay hold upon the cords of the Sektet boat, and they come in peace; the gods of the hidden place who dwell in Amentet triumph.

*******PAUSE 1 Minute for Silent Meditation*******

Play sistrum in pattern of three shakes three times (123-123-123) then continue

Pert M Heru CHAPTER 8[7]

A Conversation Between Asar _____ and God in the Form of Atum(24)[8]

1. These are the words which when spoken and understood protect an aspirant from dying a second time. These words are to be spoken by Asar _____ who is Righteous of Speech.

2. Oh Djehuti! What is it that has come into being through the conflict of the children[9] of Nut?

3. They have engendered unrest, unrighteousness and have created fiends and they have slaughtered (themselves, animals and nature[10]). They have created (for themselves) fetters by their doings which render them weak.[11]

4. Give them, Oh Great Djehuti, a commandment of Atum so that their unrighteousness may not be seen, so that you will not experience that. Shorten their years; shorten their mouths because they have committed unrighteousness towards you in secret[12].

5. I am your pallet[13] and I even brought you the inkpot as well. I am not among those with hidden unrighteousness. There is no wrongdoing within me!

6. These words are spoken by me: "Oh Atum, I am Asar _____! Tell me, what place[14] is this that I have come to? There is no water here. There is no air and there is a great darkness."

7. In this plane you have no physical body, therefore, you may live here through peace of heart. Moreover, there is no sexuality here, in place of water, air, bread, beer and lovemaking, I have given you the opportunity to attain the state of Akhu[15] together with peace of heart.

8. Atum has decreed that my face should be seen and that I should not suffer the things that cause pain.

9. Every god is sending his throne to the leader of eternity. It is thy throne, given to thy son Heru. Atum, holding what was sent to him by the elder divinities commanded this. It is he who has been ruling thy throne. It is he inheriting the throne within the island of double fire.[16] Command that I may be seen, as I am his double and that my face may see the face of Lord Atum.

10. What is the duration of life?

11. It has been decreed for millions of millions of years of duration. It is given to me to send the old ones. After that period of time I am going to destroy all created things.

12. It is the earth that came forth from Nun, now coming forth into its former state.[17]

13. I am fated with Asar; done for me to become images of the serpents, not knowing they the people and not knowing the gods and goddesses the excellent beauty that I made for Asar which was greater than all the gods and goddesses. I gave to him the desert. His son Heru is his heir on his throne within the island of

double fire.

14. I made, also, a divine ruling place for him in the Divine Boat of Millions of Years.

15. It is Heru, who is now established on the Serek[18] for those who are beloved and who are attaining sturdiness. Furthermore, the soul of Set, which is greater than all the gods and goddesses, was sent. It is given to me to make fettered his soul within the Divine Boat, for his desire is feared by divine body parts.

16. Hail father mine, Asar; do make for me what you did for thy father Ra, the achievement of long life on earth, achieving the throne, health, progeny and endurance for my tomb, and my loved ones who are on earth.

17. Grant that my enemies be destroyed, that the scorpion goddess may be on top of them, fettering them. Father mine, Ra make thee for me these things: Ankh, Udja, Seneb (*life, vitality and health*).

18. Heru is now firmly established[19] on his Serek. Give thee movement in course of time, that of advancing towards blessedness.[20]

Closing Devotional Prayer of Aspirants:

amma su en pa neter

sauu – k su emment en pa neter

au tuanu ma qeti pa haru

"Give thyself to GOD,
keep thou thyself daily for God;
and let tomorrow be as today."

NOTES: due to lack of space the note containing additional information about the chants and recitations have not been included in this booklet. You may send regular mail or email requesting a copy of the notes for better understanding and study of the worship program..

7.

Daily Chants of Shetaut Neter and Smai Tawi for Morning, Noontime and Evening Worship
(Chant each 4 times)

1

Om Amun Ra Ptah

Om Amun Ra Ptah
(The One Divine Self manifesting and the Trinity of Witnessing Consciousness, Mind and The Physical Universe)

2

Om Asar Aset Heru

Om Asar Aset Heru
The One Divine Self manifesting and the Trinity of the Divine Father, Mother and Child

3

Om Maati Maakheru

Om Maati Maakheru
The One Divine Self manifesting as the dual goddesses of truth of above and below (Heaven and Earth) Assist me in attaining spiritual enlightenment.

4

amma su en pa neter sauu - k su emment en
pa neter au tuanu ma qeti pa haru
Give thyself to GOD; keep thou thyself daily for God; and let tomorrow be as today.

5

HTP di si neter iri mettu wadj
An offering is made to propitiate that God may make the vascular system flourish
(An invocation of Health)

6

Dua Ra Dua Ra Dua Ra Khepera

Adorations to Ra, Adorations to Ra in the form of the Creator
```
Drumming Notation DD tktkt DD tktk - FAST
```

7

Dua Asar

Dua Asar Unefer Neteraah (Adorations to Asar- Pure Existence, Exalted Divinity)
Dua Asar Her Abdu (Adorations to Asar- Innermost essence of Abdu City of God)
Dua Asar Neb Djeta (Adorations to Asar- Lord of Forever)
Dua Asar Suten Heh! (Adorations to Asar- King of Eternity)
```
Drumming Notation  Beat #1 DD t   DD t   DD t   DD t - Slow
Beat #2 DD tk D - SLOW
```

8

Net Net

Net Net Dua Net Goddess Net, Goddess Net, Adorations to Goddess Net
Sefek Cheras Senhu – S Remove your vail so that I may see your true form (creation Unveiled-to see the Divine Self, i.e. spiritual enlightenment)
```
Drumming Notation  D tk DD tk DD tk DD tk - FAST
```

9

Dua Hetheru Neteritaah

Dua Hetheru Neteritaah
Adorations to Hetheru the Great Goddess.
```
Drumming Notation  D DD D DD D DD D DD - SLOW
```

10

Maat Ankhu

Maat Ankhu Maat	Maat is the source of life
Maat neb bu ten	Maat is in everywhere you are
Cha hena Maat	Rise in the morning with Maat

Ankh hena Maat   Live with Maat
Ha sema Maat   Let every limb join with Maat
(i.e. let her guide your actions)

Song Ending chant:

Dua Maat neb bu ten

Adorations to goddess Maat, who is in everywhere you are!
Drumming Notation D DDD tk - FAST

Next Steps in the Divine Worship Program

8.   *Divine Singing* – *Choose one or **more song(s) (as time allows) form the song list to listen to and sing along with

9.   *Listening* to the teachings- *read 1 Ancient Egyptian Proverb and/or **as time allows choose from a scripture or book which explains the scripture or listen to prerecorded tape of lecture on the teachings of the scriptures.

10.   *Reflection* what you have heard and record your thoughts and notes in your journal. (5 minutes-short program)

11.   *Meditation:* spend time in practice of the Glorious Light Meditation discipline allowing the mind to be at peace, realizing that what you have heard and reflected upon will lead you to expanded consciousness and enlightenment. (5 minutes-minimum for short program)

*short program, **extended program

Meditation- The Glorious Light Meditation System of Shetaut Neter*

Basic Instructions for the Glorious Light Meditation System- Given in the Tomb of Seti I. (1350 B.C.E.)

Formal meditation consists of four basic elements: Posture, Sound (chant-words of power), Visualization, Rhythmic Breathing (calm, steady breath). The instructions, translated from the original hieroglyphic text in the Tomb of Seti I contain the basic elements for formal meditation.

(1)-Posture and Focus of Attention - facing the sun

iuf iri-f ahau maq b-phr nty hau iu
body do make stand, within the Sundisk (circle of Ra)

Instruction: This means that the aspirant should remain established (sitting or lying down) as if in the center of a circle with a dot in the middle. Make your posture facing east or north.

(2)- Words of power-chant

Instruction: Utter the following hekau repeatedly during your practice

Nuk Hekau (I am the word* itself)
Nuk Ra Akhu (I am Ra's Glorious Shinning** Spirit)
Nuk Ba Ra (I am the soul of Ra)
Nuk Hekau (I am the God who creates*** through sound)
`

(3)- Visualization

Iuf   mi Ra heru mestu-f   n-shry   chet
"My body is like Ra's on the day of his birth

Instruction: visualize a golden white light at the base of your spine. As you breath in utter the hekau and visualize that the light rises up your spine to the point between your eyebrows. Then as you breath out utter the hekau again and visualize that the light is moving back down to the base of your spine. This is one cycle. Continue this practice for at least 15 minutes.

12. Closing Invocation- Chant Om-Htp, Htp, Htp,Htp, (Divine Self-Peace, Peace, Peace, Peace.)

*For more on the Glorious Light Meditation System see the book *The Glorious Light* by Sebai Muata Ashby Also available as recording on cassette and CD

DEVOTIONAL MUSIC AND THEATER OF ANCIENT EGYPT

Many people believe that the art of theater began with the ancient Greek theater. Thespis, the first actor-dramatist (About 560 B.C.E.), is considered to have been the first person to give the Greek drama its form and actors are still called "thespians." However, upon closer examination it must be noted that just as Greek philosophers such as Thales and Pythagoras learned their wisdom from the Ancient Egyptians and then set up their schools of philosophy in Greece, it is likely that the first Greek actors and playwrights learned their profession from the Ancient Egyptian Sages when they came from Greece to learn the religion and the sciences. (see the book "From Egypt to Greece") Actually, a great debt is owed to the Greek writers of ancient times because their records attest to many details which the Ancient Egyptians did not record.

There was no public theater in Ancient Egypt as the modern world knows theater at present. Theater in present day society is performed publicly for the main purpose of entertainment but in Ancient Egypt the theatrical performances were reserved for the temple exclusively. This was because the performing arts, including music, were held to be powerful and sacred endeavors which were used to impart spiritual teachings and evoke spiritual feeling and were not to be used as frivolous forms of entertainment. The Greek writer, Strabo, relates that multitudes of people would flock to festival centers (important cities and temples) where the scenes from myths related to the gods and goddesses would be acted out.

Sometimes the main episodes of the religious dramas (the most esoteric elements were performed in the interior portion of the temple for initiates, priests and priestesses only) were performed outside the temple, in the courtyard or between the pylons and were the most important attraction of the festivals. (see the temple diagram) The priests and priestesses took great care with costumes and the decorations (direction and set design). The spectators knew the myths that were being acted out but never stopped enjoying their annual performance, being a retelling of the divine stories, which bring purpose and meaning to life. Thus, the art of acting was set aside for spiritual purposes and was not to be used for mindless entertainment, which serves only to distract the mind from reality and truth. The spectators would take part by clapping, lamenting at sad parts and crying out with joy and celebrating when the ultimate triumph came. In this manner the spectators became part of the myth and the myth is essentially the life of the gods and goddesses and their lives are what not only sustains the world, but also what leads to understanding the connection between the physical, material and spiritual worlds. Further, the occasions were used as opportunities for enjoying life, though it was understood to be fleeting. Thus, the bridge between the mortal world and the eternal world was established, through mythological drama and the performing arts.

In the Ancient Egyptian view, life cannot be enjoyed without affirming the Divine, the Spirit. Further, theater, religion and mystical philosophy were considered to be aspects of the same discipline, known as "Shetaut Neter" or the "mysteries" or "Yoga Sciences." Every aspect of life in Ancient Egypt was permeated by the awareness and inclusion of spiritual philosophy. For example. lawyers and judges followed the precepts of Maat and medical doctors followed and worshipped the teachings of the god Djehuti, who was adopted by the Greeks as the god Asclapius. This idea is also evident in the Ancient Egyptian manner of saying grace before meals even by ordinary householders. Prior to consuming food, the host of an ordinary household would invite the guests to view an image of a divinity, principally Asar (Osiris) the god of the afterlife, thereby reminding the guests that life is fleeting, even as they are about to enjoy a sumptuous meal. In this manner, a person is reminded of the ultimate fate of life and a reflective state of mind is engendered rather than an arrogant and egoistic state. This theme is present in every aspect of Ancient Egyptian culture at its height.

The Ancient Egyptian Sages instituted tight controls on theater and music because the indulgence in inappropriate entertainments was known to cause mental agitation and undesirable behaviors. The famous Greek Philosopher and student of the Ancient Egyptian Mysteries, Pythagoras, wrote that the Ancient Egyptians placed particular attention to the study of music. Another famous Greek Philosopher and student of the Ancient Egyptian Mysteries, Plato, states that they thought it was beneficial to the youths. Strabo confirms that music was taught to youths along with reading and writing, however, it was understood that music meant for entertainment alone was harmful to the mind, making it agitated and difficult to control oneself, and thus was strictly controlled by the state and the priests and priestesses. Like the sages of India, who instituted Nada Yoga, or the spiritual path of music, the Ancient Egyptians held that music was of Divine origin and as such was a sacred endeavor. The Greek writer, Athenaeus, informs us that the Greeks and barbarians from other countries learned music from the Ancient Egyptians. Music was so important in Ancient Egypt that professional musicians were contracted and kept on salaries at the temples. Music was considered important because it has the special power to carry the mind to either elevated (spiritual) states or (worldly) states. When there is overindulgence in music for entertainment and escapism (tendency to desire to escape from daily routine or reality by indulging in fantasy, daydreaming, or entertainment) the mind is filled with worldly impressions, cravings, lusting, and uncontrolled urges. In this state of mind, the capacity for right thinking and feeling are distorted or incapacitated. The advent of audio and visual recording technology and their combinations in movies and music videos, is more powerful because the visual element, coupled with music, and the ability to repeat with intensity of volume, acts to intoxicate the mind with illusory and fantasy thoughts. The body is also affected in this process. The vibrations of the music and the feelings contained in it through the lyrics and sentiment of the performer evokes the production of certain bio-chemical processes in the mind and body. This capacity of music is evident in movies musicals, converts, audio recordings, etc., in their capacity to change a persons mood. Any and all messages given to the mind affect it and therefore great care should be taken to fill the mind with the right kinds of messages in the form of ideas and feelings.

Those societies which produce and consume large quantities of audio and audio-visual entertainment for non-spiritual purposes will exhibit the greatest levels of mental agitation, violence, individual frustration, addiction, mental illness, physical illness, etc., no matter how materially prosperous or technologically advanced they may become. So true civilization and success of a society should not be judged by material prosperity or technological advancement but rather how successful it is in producing the inner fulfillment of its citizens. Being the creators of and foremost practitioners of Maat Philosophy (adherence to the principles of righteousness in all aspects of life*), the Ancient Egyptians created a culture which existed longer (at least 5,000 years) than any other known society. Therefore, the real measures of civilization and human evolution are to be discerned by the emphasis on and refinement of the performing and visual arts and spiritual philosophy, for these endeavors serve to bring harmony to the individual and to society. It should be clearly understood that art should not become stagnant or rigid in its expression since this is the means by which it is renewed for the understanding of new generations. Rather, the principles contained in the arts should be kept intact in the performance of the rituals, paintings, sculptures, music, etc. since these reflect transcendental truths which are effective today as they were 5,000 years ago in the Ancient Egyptian temple and will be effective until the end of time. The loss of these is the cause of disharmony in society but societal dysfunction is in reality only a reflection of disharmony in the individual human heart which has lost its connection with the higher Self within. (*See the book "The Wisdom of Maati." **The word spiritual here implies any endeavor which seeks to bring understanding about the ultimate questions of life: Who am I and What is life all about. So spirituality may or may not be related to organized religion.)

Thus, the question of whether or not music and entertainment has an effect on youth and the mind of a person was resolved in ancient times. The Ancient Egyptians observed that the people from Greece and the Asiatic countries were more aggressive and that their behavior was unstable.* They attributed these problems to their lifestyle, which was full of strife due to life in harsh geographical regions, meat eating and overindulgence in sense pleasures, or the inability to control the human urges and the consequent disconnection from the natural order of the universe as well as their spiritual inner selves. These observations of the psychology and lifestyle of the foreigners prompted the Ancient Egyptian Sages to refer to the Greeks and Asiatics (Middle Easterners) as "children" and "miserable"..."barbarians." Their observations allowed the Ancient Egyptian Sages to create a philosophy of life and a psycho-spiritual environment wherein the Egyptian people could grow and thrive in physical, mental and spiritual health. (See the books Egyptian Yoga Vol. 1 and 2 and The 42 Laws of Maat and the Wisdom Texts)

In Ancient Greece, theater became a practice which was open to the public and later on in the Christian era it deteriorated into mindless entertainment or a corrupted endeavor of con artists and in present times it is a big business wherein its participants are paid excessive and disproportionately high salaries for their entertainment skills; or otherwise said, their ability to sell merchandise. In modern times the almost unfettered creation and promotion of movies, videos, music and other forms of entertainment containing elements designed to promote sense pleasures and excitement, leads to mental agitation but with little true satisfaction of the inner need of the heart. Thus, while the entertainments may cause excitation they do not lead to abiding fulfillment and inner peace, but to more desires for more excitement in a never ending cycle which is impossible to fulfill. This process leads to mental confusion and stress which in turn lead to strife and conflict, internal frustration. Corresponding with the emergence of Western and Middle Eastern culture, with its negative lifestyle elements noted by the Ancient Egyptians, the world has also seen an increase in wars, violence against women, children, environmental destruction, enslavement and taking advantage of weaker human beings, drug abuse, crime, divorce, and overall personal dissatisfaction with life. In other words, the lack of restraints, both individuals and in societies as a whole, has led to frustration with life, a kind of cultural depression and degradation, which has led to record numbers of people suffering from mental illnesses such as depression, schizophrenia, psychosis, as well as medical disorders of all kinds which were not present in ancient times due to self-control and the direction of life being guided by spiritual pursuits as opposed to egoistic pursuits. The Ancient Egyptian Mystery theater provides the means for allowing a human being to come into harmony with the spiritual reality (mental expansion and self-discovery) while frivolous entertainment serves to dull the intellectual capacity to discover and understand anything beyond the physical world and the physical sense pleasures of life (mental contraction and hardening of the ego). This inability to go beyond sense pleasures and experiences the world of human activity is what leads a person to mental stress which in turn leads to mental illness and physical illness.

Devotional spiritual practice is closely related to singing and chanting the divine names. Its purpose is to purify the heart and to lead one to a harmony of mind and body so as to allow a spiritual awakening and a spiritual realization. Divine Singing is the science of sound and the art of playing music in such a manner as to lead the mind to transcendental forms of spiritual ecstasy and oneness with the Divine. The following musical compositions have been recorded and are available on quality Compact Disc formats. They have presented the original-traditional form as well as have successfully integrated the ancient melodies and devotional music with Jazz, Reggae, Pop and other musical forms. This collection explores this musical form but also incorporating the music and philosophy of ancient Africa, using the chants of the ancient Egyptian hieroglyphic texts. This combination of music is designed to show the complementary nature of Kamitan culture and spiritual philosophy and to uplift any student of Ancient African music and Divine Worship.

This production made use of reproductions of Ancient Egyptian musical instruments and modern musical instruments as well as modern western musical instruments.

KEMETIC Divine Singing

Sebai Maa (Dr. Muata Ashby) began his research into the spiritual philosophy of ancient Egypt (Kemet or Kamit) and noticed that the teachings correlated to what is today referred to as mysticism and yoga. This was the catalyst for a successful book series on the subject called "Egyptian Yoga". Now he has created a series of musical compositions which explore this unique area of music from ancient Egypt and its connection to world music. Sebai Maa is the only exponent of Ancient Egyptian Music incorporating the ancient Hekau or Ancient Egyptian (Kemetic) words of power in a musical form for devotional spiritual practice, dancing, or pure listening pleasure.

"Devote yourself to adore God's name."

—Ancient Egyptian Proverb

Music has the capacity to bring us into balance with the cosmos and God is that same Divine essence. Music is a devotional exercise that carries our feelings up to the divine realms and thus leads us to spiritual enlightenment when it is dedicated to the Divine with a spiritual intent.

Singing God's name or chanting God's name is the way prescribed by sages and saints the world over, for changing the vibrations of one's personality and the environment, achieving mental peace and coming closer to the Divine!

The following are the lyrics for the Kemetic devotional songs prepared by Dr. Muata Ashby.

Below: Sebai Muata Ashby and Sba Dja Ashby conducting a Divine Singing Session

KEMETIC MUSIC COLLECTION

The following are descriptions of the contents of the music CD collections based on Kamitan Culture and Neterian Spirituality

From the CD: Adorations to Ra and Hetheru:

"Adorations to Ra and Hetheru" is a compilation of musical notions engendered by the exploration of Ancient Egyptian musical instruments and musical theory. *Merit* is the ancient Egyptian goddess of music and as a follower of Aset (Isis) and as an artist, I felt especially inspired by her throughout the production of these melodies and rhythms.

May the blessings of Merit be on all who listen to this music!

1- **Dua Ra Cheft Uben F** (Adorations to Ra When he rises)

Dua Ra Cheft Uben F is a direct translation of the first section of the Hymn to Ra contained in the Pert Em Hru or Book of Coming Forth By Day of Any. Ra is the Supreme Being, like God the Father in Christianity, or Allah in Islam. This song was written with a meditative, devotional attitude and was designed for playing especially at dawn.

Instruments used: Nefer, Sistrum, Cymbals, Drone Choir. It is translated:

Dua Ra Cheft Uben F em aket abdet ent Pet
Adorations to Ra When he rises in horizon eastern
Anetej Ra-k iti em Khepera
Homage to Ra, coming forth as Khepera
Khepera qemam neteru
Khepera, Creator of the gods and goddesses
Cha – k uben – k pesd Mut – k
Rising thee, shinning thee, lighting up thy mother
Cha ti em suten neteru
Rising as Lord, king of the gods and goddesses
Iri – nek mut Nut aiui – em iri nini

Your mother Nut does an act of worship to you with both arms

Manu em hetep hept-tu Maat er tra

Manu (Western Horizon) receives thee in peace, Maat embraces thee at the double season (perennially)
(Translation by Dr. Muata Ashby)

2- Dua Ra, Dua Ra, Dua Ra Khepera

Dua Ra Khepera means Adorations to Ra in the form of Khepera. These words of power are based on the mythology related to the Supreme Being who manifests in the Ra-Khepera, the Creator, the form of the morning sun which creates the day or brings it into being with his rising. Its attitude is lively, exciting and devotional, designed for late morning listening. Instruments used: Vocals, Nefer, Sistrum, Clapping, and Tar.

Drumming Notation DD tktkt DD tktk - FAST

3- Dua Hetheru Neterit-aah (Adorations to Hathor, the Great Goddess)

Dua Hetheru Neterit-aah means Adorations to Hathor, the great goddess. It was written in the Dorian Mode. It is a devotional to the goddess in her form as the great mistress of the universe. It was written in an expansive mood, feeling the glory of the Divine and the warmth of the feminine aspect of the Divine. The long commencement of the song with the sistrum is a homage to the goddess as it is her special musical instrument, used to awaken the *Arat* serpent power (known as Kundalini) in Indian mysticism. Instruments used: Vocal, Nefer, Sistrum, Tar, Drone Choir. *Dua Hetheru Neterit-aah* is the first line in a poem written by Muata Ashby based on the mythology of goddess Hetheru.

Dua Hetheru Neterit-aah (Adorations to Hathor, the Great Goddess)
Dua Hetheru Sekhem-aah (Adorations to Hathor, the Great Power)
Dua Hetheru Nebt Tawii (Adorations to Hathor, the Mistress of the Earth)
Dua Hetheru Sat Nesu Ra (Adorations to Hathor, the Daughter of King Ra)

4- Dua Hetheru Sekhem aah

Dua Hetheru Neterit-aah means Adorations to Hathor, the great goddess of Life Force Power. In Ancient Egyptian the term *Sekhem* means Life Force energy, like the Chi of the Chinese and Prana of the Indian Yoga mystics. In her aspect as Sekhmet, Hetheru displays her power in much the same way as the goddess Durga displays her power in her aspect as of Kali. This song was performed in the Phrygian mode. It is *Lively, exciting and devotional*. Instruments used: Vocal, Nefer, Sistrum, Cymbals, Tar, Drone Choir. It has a driving beat that extols the energy of the goddess. Instruments used: Vocal, Nefer, Sistrum, Cymbals, Tar, Drone Choir.

5- Amma su em Pa Neter (Give Thyself to God)

Amma su em Pa Neter is a passage from the Ancient Egyptian Wisdom texts. It was an injunction written by Sage Any. The complete texts reads:

Amma su en Pa Neter

sauu – k su emment en Pa Neter

au duanu ma qedi pa haru

"Give thyself to The GOD,

keep thou thyself daily for The God;

and let tomorrow be as today."

It was conceived as being a devotional injunction of wisdom which must be reflected upon and then put into action. Therefore, the first three quarters of the song is performed in the *Slow, meditative and devotional* mode. The last quarter was performed in the *Lively, exciting and devotional* mode. Instruments used: Vocal, Nefer, Sistrum, Cymbals, Tar, Clapping, Drone Choir.

6- Drum Circle of Maat

The Drum Circle of Maat was conceived by means of reflections on the goddess in the form of Maat. Maat is the aspect of the goddess symbolizing order, righteousness, truth, stamina, non-violence, etc. She sits at the bow of the Barque of Ra, making a way so that it may traverse the heavens and engender Creation. She enables Khepera's Creation. As with all sea voyages, sometimes there is smooth sailing. At other times there are squalls and even storms and tidal waves. These variations (prosperity and adversity in life-ups and downs) are symbolized by the four separate drum beats produced in this piece. Beginning with one beat the others join in. They are all different and sometimes they seem discordant but there is still a commonality which brings harmony and works through the discordance. With this harmony established the movement of Maat forges ahead, reaching its conclusion in the dissolution which will enable a new creation to come forth. The Drum Circle of Maat was performed in the *Lively, exciting and devotional* mode. Instruments used: Sistrum, Cymbals, Tar.

7- Nefer solo with scale vocal introduction.

The Nefer solo with scale vocal introduction was conceived in the *Slow, meditative and devotional* mode. It is one of a series of personal muses of contemplations between musician and instrument. It is part of a continuing investigation of the player's and instrument's relation as well as a tribute to the creators and their intent in creating it and playing it. In ancient times the Nefer was considered sacred to the God Asar, as it was the only musical instrument not banned from his burial sites. Nefer means that which is beautiful and good. If the instrument is played well it can bring forth what is most beautiful in life, a harmony between spirit and matter, soul and God, above and below, etc. Instruments used: Vocals, Nefer.

8- Heru's Triumphant March

Heru's Triumphant March was inspired by the divinity, Horus or Heru in his form as Heruakuti. Heruakuti means Heru of the two horizons. He is all encompassing and formidable as well as irresistible. The martial character of this piece was well intended as it relates to the determination and power that is contained in this aspect of the Divine. In Ancient Egypt and to present day followers of the Kemetic (Egyptian) path to spiritual enlightenment the various forms of divinities or the gods and goddesses are not understood as separate and distinct entities but as aspects of the Supreme Divinity. They are as emanations of the singular Supreme essence which gives life to all things. So Kemetic religion is not polytheistic but, like Hinduism, it is monotheistic in its higher application and monistic in its specialized mystical application. Instruments used: Sistrum, Cymbals, Nefer and Tar.

Vocals: Muata Ashby, Karen "Dja" Ashby (on Dua Ra Khepera), Sistrums: Muata Ashby, Cymbals: Muata Ashby, Nefer: Muata Ashby, Clapping: Muata Ashby, Tar: Muata Ashby.

The Following songs are in the CD: *Om Asar, Aset Heru*

1-*Om Asar Aset Heru Part 1* (The Divine Self Manifesting as the Glorious Trinity: Osiris, Isis and Horus)– 6:05 – M. Ashby

> *Om Asar Aset Heru* (The Self as Osiris, Isis and Horus)
> *Ha Asar, Ha Aset Ha Heru* (Hail Osiris, Isis and Horus)
> *Dua, Dua, Dua* (Adorations thrice)
> *Neb Asar, Nebt Aset, Heqa Heru* (Lord (King) Osiris, Queen Isis, Prince Horus)
> *Nebt Aset, Rekat Aset* (Queen Isis, Mistress of Wisdom)
> *Rekat nehast Asar, Rekat nehast Heru* (Isis, the mistress of wisdom resurrected Osiris and Horus)

In Ancient Egypt, as in India, **"Om"** means the singular transcendental essence, the name of God. Asar was considered as God the Father in Christianity, Allah in Islam or Shiva in India. With his wife Aset and his son Heru, they formed a great Trinity of spirituality. Their story constitutes the great myth known as the Ausarian Resurrection, the life, death and resurrection of Asar (Osiris) which later inspired the Christian resurrection as well as that of other religions which came later. This song was performed in the Festival mode, being in the *Lively, exciting and devotional* form. Its inspiration came from the visualization of a festivity in dedication of Asar (Osiris), Aset (Isis), and Heru (Horus). Instruments used: Vocal, Nefer, Sistrum, Cymbals, Clapping, Tar.

2-Dua Asar-Adorations to Asar-Asar's Party – 6:19 – M. Ashby

This song was inspired by two forces. The first was the great hymns to Asar from Kamit (Ancient Egypt), in particular, the one contained in the Pert Em Heru or Book of Coming Forth By Day (Book of the Dead) in the papyrus of Any. The second force that inspired this song was the visualization of Asar' who was fond of parties and festivities, like the god Shiva of India, dancing with complete immersion and intoxication with his own glory, which reflects in creation. The lyrics are:

Dua Asar Unfr Ntr aah hr ab Abdu
Adorations to Asar, Divinity great, innermost heart of Abydos*
Suten Heh Nb Djtah
King of Eternity, Lord of Forever
Sbbebi heh m aha djtah
Spanning millions of years in his rising
Se dp n chat Nut
Son, eldest from the body of Nut
Ut-t n Geb, r-pat neb ur-rt
Begotten by Geb, the foremost Lord of the ureret crown.

Translated by Muata Ashby *Sacred city of Asar Instruments used: Vocal, Nefer, Sistrum, Cymbals, Clapping, Tar.

3-Set's Desire – 6:13 –M. Ashby

Set was Asar's younger brother. His greed caused him to murder Asar, who was the king of Egypt. Therefore, this song was performed in a lively mode, like that experienced by an agitated mind, going every which way, not knowing how to find satisfaction. It makes use of discordant notes on the Nefer guitar to convey the discordance of Set's unrighteous and egoistic desires. This piece actually has two parts. The second part conveys a more controlled expression, the harmonizing and calming of the agitated mind. The agitation of mind from unrighteous thoughts and feelings is the mental defect which leads to mental disturbance, violence, anger, hatred, jealousy, etc. in life. This song is designed to calm the agitated mind. Instruments used: Nefer, Vocal, Tar.

4-Tears of Aset – 8:13–M. Ashby

Tears of Aset was inspired by the Ancient Egyptian myth known as the "Ausarian Resurrection." In it, Set conspired to kill Asar's son so that there would be no contender for the throne of Asar. Set sent a scorpion to kill Heru and succeeded. When Aset discovered this she wept bitterly and this song is my expression of those tears and the sorrow which she felt. To me the Nefer guitar was the only instrument which could convey this mood. The second part of the song rises out of melancholy. It comes back with a determination to do something in order to reverse the great loss. Heru was the hope of all to challenge Set and restore order and righteous rule to the land. So goddess Aset cried and experienced her grief but determined to fight on. Instruments used: Nefer, Sistrum, Cymbals, Tar.

5-Escape into the Papyrus Swamps-5:02–M. Ashby

Determined to escape the evil of Set, the goddess ran into the papyrus swamps to save herself and her son. The movement in this song begins as a lively but orderly stepping movement down a path. But as the myth relates, Set found her and determined to kill her and then the movement becomes rapid and almost frantic, like a person running away from a mugger. But eventually she finds safety and a place to recuperate and pray for assistance. Instruments used: Nefer, Sistrum, Tar.

6-Neferti– Double Beauty, the Dance of Asar and Aset – 8:20–M. Ashby
Neferti refers to Nefer in plural. It has two meanings here, Nefer relating to the use of two guitars and also the visualization of the two divinities, Asar and Aset, coming together, reunited after she brought him back from death after being killed by Set. They are doing the dance of life on the dance floor of eternity as the drum and the two guitars express their joy and love for each other. One of the guitars performs an unchanging pattern, this one is Asar. The other moves, places ornaments of sound and improvises on the first and sometimes even matches, harmonizes with it. In tantric philosophy the male is the immovable spirit and the female is the active element. Thus this is a song designed with sensuousness, joy and spiritual ecstasy. This is Ancient Egyptian Tantra Yoga. Instruments used: Nefer, Sistrum, Cymbals, Tar.

7-Om Yaah-Supplication to the Moon Djehuti-5:30–M. Ashby

This song was inspired by the time when the goddess was holding the dead body of her child, Heru, in her arms. After crying she began to call out to the heavens for help and help did come in the form of the god Djehuti, whose symbol is the moon., Yaah. The legendary description of this call is that it was of such intent quality that the boat of Ra came to a halt and with it time came to a halt also. In this period beyond time Heru was healed. This supplication is what every spiritual aspirant must be able to do in order to receive divine assistance. Instruments used: Vocal, Chorus Drone in Sa-Pa (D and A).

8-Akhu Anetg Aset– Glory and Homage to Goddess Aset – 6:41 –M. Ashby

This song is a poem I wrote to the goddess. It was a great pleasure for me since the goddess is my personal devotional path. In particular, the forms of Sekhmet and Aset are my favorites. This song is devoted to Aset, the goddess of wisdom, whose words of power resurrected Asar and also had the intensity to stop time and call the spirit down to earth to resurrect her son, Heru. If a spiritual aspirant learns the words of power of goddess Aset he or she will attain Nehast or resurrection (spiritual enlightenment). Instruments used: Vocal, Sistrum, Cymbals, Clapping, Chorus, Tar. The lyrics are:

Akhu, Akhu (Glory, Glory)
Anetg Nbt Tawi (Homage to the mistress (Queen) of the land)
Arti aah m hekau (Goddess great in words of power)
Dua Aset, Neterit aah Aset (Adorations to Aset, Goddess great, Aset)
Dua Aset nehast Asar (Adorations to Aset, who resurrected Asar)
Dua Aset, Mut Heru ((Adorations to Aset, mother of Horus)
Dua Aset, Sehu Heru (Adorations to Aset, Spiritual Preceptor of Horus)
Dua Aset, Neru Aset (Adorations to Aset, victorious Aset)

Drumming Notation DD DDtktktk DD DDtktktk – Fast

9-Nut's Expansion – 7:05 –M. Ashby

This version of the song is actually part two of the entire composition. Part 1 will appear in a future CD. This part was chosen for this CD because of its meditative qualities. Nut's expansion is an exploration of infinity and eternity. She is the mother of Aset and Asar she also gives birth to the sun every morning. She also allows souls to rise up to the heavens but those souls must come in hetep (peace). Thus this song is a meditation on infinity (going beyond space), eternity (going beyond time), and Hetep (going beyond mental agitations caused by worldliness-hetep is inner spiritual peace and contentment). Instruments used: Sistrum, Cymbals, Tar. The lyrics are:

10-Om Asar Aset Heru Part 2– 2:28 –M. Ashby
See description in track #1

(Translations by Dr. Muata Ashby)

Vocals: Muata Ashby, Sistrums: Muata Ashby, Cymbals: Muata Ashby, Nefer: Muata Ashby, Clapping: Muata Ashby, Tar: Muata Ashby.
Copyright 1999 Muata Ashby

The Following Songs are in the CD: Haari Om

On the CD cover left- the God Heru of Ancient Egypt-Nefertem siting on the primeval lotus of creation. Right- the God Brahma-(sometimes called Krishna) of India, siting on the primeval lotus of creation. "Haari Om" is a compilation of musical notions engendered by the exploration of Ancient Egyptian musical instruments and musical theory as well as Indian devotional music.

The Ancient Egyptian Word "Haari"

Amun (Hidden essence of creation-witnessing consciousness)

The title was chosen because it typifies my feeling about the connection between Ancient Egypt and India in ancient times. In my book *Egyptian Yoga Volume I,* I was able to show that in Ancient Egypt two of the divine names of God that were used are "Am" and "Om".[21] These are the same as the Indian "Aum" and "Om". I also showed the cultural and mythological correlations between the two countries and how the spiritual philosophies are kindred. It was derived from the name of the god Amun. Similarly, the Christian Amen and the Jewish Shalom are derivatives. However, the word "Haari" was also used in Ancient Egypt as a "Hekau" or Divine Word of Power. In India, "Hari" signifies the Divine name of Lord Krishna, the "Swarthy One". Lord Krishna is known as "The Black One". Similarly, Amun of Ancient Egypt was referred to as "Black". Thus, Haari Om seemed as a perfect title for a compilation of songs which explore a fusion between the musical and spiritual arts and religion of Ancient Egypt and India.

The Indian Sanskrit Symbol "Aum" or "Om"

About the Songs in this collection:

1-*Haari Om* – Sebai Maa (M. Ashby)

This song grew out of my love for Indian devotional singing and music and a desire to meld this with Kemetic (Ancient Egyptian) musical forms. It is in essence a musical exploration of my research in the history and philosophy of Yoga and the cultures of Ancient Egypt and India and of course, my devotion to Om. Using traditional and devotional styles of vocal performance, this piece propitiates the Divine in the form of the Ancient Egyptian and East Indian Words of Power. It is meant to open up the feeling aspect of the personality through the sometimes harmonious and at other times almost wailing form of singing. Through all of this, the organic, driving beat, as a mixture of Middle Eastern, African and Indian forms, carries us to a union with Om and Om is the Divine.

Drumming Notation DDDDD t t DDDDD t t

Haari Om Tat Sat!

2- *Fusion: Ancient Egypt Meets India* – Sebai Maa

Fusion is a melding of Kemetic feeling with Indian feeling. It blends Ancient Egyptian and East Indian musical instruments in order to create a harmonious groove that is at the same time engaging, calming and also exiting as well as meditative. Through the surreal pulsating, regular beat it is designed for meditation or easy listening with the purpose of calming the mind but stimulating a positive mode of feeling and thinking which occurs when the lower feelings and thoughts of the mind are sublimated and developed into higher spiritual energies.

3-*Hetheru Aha* – Sebai Maa

Hetheru aha is based on the Ancient Egyptian story of the goddess Hetheru (Hathor) and Djehuti (Thoth). It was originally created to be sung at a point in a stage-play I wrote (***The Journey of Hetheru***) where Hetheru is discouraged and spiritually lost, having forgotten her true identity as a goddess. Djehuti is her spiritual preceptor, her Guru, and he sings to her the following words of wisdom to enlighten her:

Hetheru aha, m Sekhem aah ten Neteritaa
Hetheru, raise yourself up in your true form as the great goddess of Power (Life Force)

Ten Nebetawi, Ten Neberdjer, Uben tawi
You are the mistress of the world, you are all encompassing divinity, the light of the world

Rekhit iri, neteru iri, anetj k ren
The people on earth and the gods and goddesses all praise your name
en Nebetawi, Ten Neberdjer, ten Neterit aah nefert
You are the mistress of the world, you are all encompassing divinity, the great goddess of beauty.

Drumming Notation
MAIN   **D t DD t DD t DD - Fast**
OPPOSING-COMP   **D t D Dt D t D Dt - Fast**

This song was a continuation of the devotional music to the goddess which began in my second CD, Adorations to Ra and Hetheru). Its melody and the use of ancient and modern musical instruments bring the feeling of the goddess alive for our times. It is a joy to sing and an honor to be given the opportunity to be used as her voice. This song was inspired also by the famous festivals of Hetheru, which were the most popular festive occasions in Ancient Egyptian culture. Therefore, it is lively and suitable for singing along as well as dancing.

4- *Ram Bhajamana*– Sebai Maa

Ram Bhajamana is a devotional rendition of a chant dedicated to the Indian form of god: Rama and his consort Sita. Rama is an Avatar, an incarnation of the Supreme Self. His mission was to show the way, through righteous living, so as to attain a state of supreme blessedness. The words "Ra" and "Ma" are also special in Kemetic Yoga Mysticism. Ra means Divine Self and Ma is his daughter Maat, the order, glory and righteousness of spiritual life. The concordance and harmony of the two philosophies is unmistakable and it is our good ari (karma) to enjoy both the mystical traditions and the sum of the two

94

which is greater than either put together. Vocal: Sebai Maa, Karen "Dja" Ashby The lyrics are:

Ram Ram Bhajamana
Sing and keep the name of Ram in mind
Hare Hare Hare Ram
Hail Hail Hail to Ram
Jaya Jaya Sita Rama
Spiritual victory to Sita and Ram!
Jaya Jaya Sita Ram
Spiritual victory to Sita and Ram!

5-*Maat Ankhu* – Sebai Maa

Composed in the traditional Ancient Egyptian style, Maat Ankhu was inspired by the text of the Ancient Egyptian text now referred to as the Berlin Papyrus. As a long time student of Maat Philosophy from Ancient Egypt this song evoked the wonder and glory of knowing that the goddess (Maat) is everywhere and in anything and that if we live our lives in harmony with her by acting righteously and acknowledging the divine in every aspect of our lives we will discover the glory of spiritual enlightenment. This song is for anyone in need of support from the source of truth, righteousness and harmony. For more on the philosophy of Maat see my two books **The Wisdom of Maati** and **The 42 Precepts of Maat.** The lyrics are:

Maat Ankhu Maat
Maat is the source of life
Maat neb bu ten
Maat is in everywhere you are
Cha hena Maat
Rise in the morning with Maat
Ankh hena Maat
Live with Maat
Ha sema Maat
Let every limb join with Maat
(i.e. let her guide your actions)
Maat her ten
Maat is who you are deep down

95

(i.e. your true identity is one with the Divine)
Dua Maat neb bu ten

Adorations to goddess Maat, who is in everywhere you are!

6-*Ptah Neter Aah*— Sebai Maa

This wonderful song is based on the Ancient Egyptian Hieroglyphic text that is inscribed on a pillar that can be seen even today in the temple of Senusert I at Karnak in Egypt, Africa. It is an inscription of the Medu Neter Divine Speech of the God Ptah (one of the forms of the Supreme Being from Ancient Egypt) to the king. It affirms the devotion of the king towards the god and it affirms God's devotion towards the devotee. The first part of the composition is a recitation of the speech and then it is accompanied by the Nefer (Ancient Egyptian Lute). Then it is rendered in a modern form using modern instruments. The lyrics are:

Neter Ptah Resuanab, meduje
The God Ptah, Lord of White Wall (the city of Memphis) speaks thus

Di n ankh, djed, uas neb
I give life, spiritual stability, and all power

Seneb neb awet ab neb
All health and expansion of heart (joy)

N nesu biti, Kheper Ka Ra
To the king Kheper Ka Ra (a title of Senusert I)

Di ankh djed, uas, mi Ra
I give life, spiritual stability, and all power to be like Ra
(i.e. to be immortal, all-powerful as a radiant spirit)

Dua Ptah (Adorations to the god Ptah)

7-*Shu's Breath*– Sebai Maa

This song was inspired by thoughts of air, breeze and wind as well as breath and life force energy. Shu is the god of air and this song is a propitiation to Shu that there may be unobstructed breath, cool breeze and prosperity in health. Along with this, Shu is the god of space so the propitiation also relates to the desire to be in open spaces and to live in freedom. Performed in the traditional Ancient Egyptian mode, this piece is designed to calm the mind through its regular beat and airiness. Dua Shu (Adorations to the god Shu)

All Translations by © 1999 Sebai Maa (Dr. Muata Ashby)
Vocals: Muata Ashby, Sistrums: Muata Ashby, Cymbals: Muata Ashby, Nefer: Muata Ashby, Clapping: Muata Ashby, Tar: Muata Ashby.

The Following Songs are in the CD: Ra Akhu

Track 2: ***Dua heru*** -Adorations to Heru

Dua Heru (Adorations to Heru)
Dua Heru (Adorations to Heru)
Dua Heru (Adorations to Heru)
Suten Heh (Lord of Eternity)

Dua Heru Sa Asar Aset
Adorations to Heru, the son of Asar and Aset

Dua Heru Aha Maat
Adorations to Heru, he stands for righteousness and truth

Dua Heru Uben Tawi
Adorations to Heru, he is the light of the world

Dua Heru nestu tawi
Adorations to Heru, he is the king of kings.

Track 4: ***Dua Ankh Herakuti:*** Hymn to Ated by Akhenaten:

Dua Ankh Herakhuti Ha m Akhet
Adorations to the living Horus in the two horizons, residing in the horizon
M ren-f m Shu m Aten
In his name of Shu in the form of the Sundisk
Di ankh djeta heh
Giving life forever and for eternity
In suten ankh m Maat Neb Tawi
This praise is sung by the king (Akhenaten), the living, in righteousness,
Lord of the two lands (Ancient Egypt)
Nefer Kheperu Ra ua n Ra
The good king in his name Creator, one with God

Drumming Notation D t tktD D t tktD

Track 5: ***Nuk Ra Khu*** I am Ra's Glorious Shining Spirit

The Hekau prescribed by the ancient Egyptian Sages for use with the Glorious Light Meditation, based on the Ancient Egyptian Scripture:

Nuk Hekau (I am the word* itself)
Nuk Ra Akhu (I am Ra's Glorious Shinning** Spirit)
Nuk Ba Ra (I am the soul of Ra)
Nuk Hekau (I am the God who creates*** through sound)
Drumming Notation D tkt DD t - SLOW

Copyright 1999 Sebai Maa (Muata Ashby)

The Following songs are from the CD Glories of the Divine Mother

"Glories of the Divine Mother" is a compilation of musical notions engendered by the exploration of Ancient Egyptian musical instruments and musical theory. It is based on the original Ancient Egyptian hieroglyphic text praising the goddess Net who is a prototype for the goddess Aset (Isis). All lyrics were translated based on the text directly as well as other texts extolling the powers of the goddess.

May the blessings of Merit be on all who
listen to this music!

About the Songs:

Glories of the Great Mother
Music based on he teachings of the Ancient Egyptian Goddess Net

Track 1 Ya Mut Ur

This song is based entirely on an adoration text dedicated to the goddess Net. It is a praise of the goddess, recognizing her transcendental and unfathomable nature. The lyrics are:

Ya Mut Ur an Sefech Mesu-s
　　Hail Great Mother, whose birth is unknown
Ya netert-aah em Duat Shetat sen
　　Hail Great Goddess who is doubly hidden in the netherworld
Ntet reck –s , Ntet reck –s
　　Not known is she, not known is she.
Ya neterit-aah Shetat sen
　　Hail Great Goddess who is doubly hidden
Drumming Notation D DD tk D DD tk D DD tk DDtD

99

Track 2 Net Net Dua Net Short Version
(Featuring the vocals of Sebai Maa and (Dja Ashby))

This song is based on the same text but is shortened to a simple chant and the music makes modern instruments and style and is designed for chanting and dancing. It is a resolution to the lyrics presented in the first song, asking the goddess to reveal herself to the spiritual aspirant.

Net Net Dua Net Sefech Cheras Senhu-s
Goddess Net, Goddess Net, loosen your clothing (i.e. reveal yourself – your glory, that is your true form)
Drumming Notation D tk DD tk DD tk DD tk - FAST

Track 3 Net Dua Net Slow R&B-Jazz Groove

This song is based on the same text of Goddess Net, emphasizing the hidden aspect of the goddess as she is "doubly" unfathomable and yet most accessible to her devotees through praise and song. It makes use of ancient and modern instruments.

Net Dua Net　　　　　(Net Adorations to Net)
Neterit Aah shetat sen (Goddess great hidden doubly)
Ya mut ur m Duat　　　(Hail mother great who is in the
　　　　Netherworld)
Ntet reck –s, ntet wat　(not know is she, or the way to her)

Track 4 Netritaah Net Jazz Groove
(Featuring the piano playing of Reginald Ashby Sr.)

This song is based on the same text encompassing her creative aspect. She is the source for all that exists and all that will come into being. She is the Supreme essence of creation. The music for this song was created with the idea of glory and sheer beauty of sound. The melody is most important as it soothes the heart and relaxes the mind, developing a flow which leads to eternity and peace in the Goddess.

Netritaah Net (Oh Great goddess Net)
M Duat shetat sen (who resides in the Netherworld hidden doubly)

Chemam neteru (She is the creator of the gods and goddesses)
Mesu Ra (She gave birth to the god Ra)

Uben tawi

Drumming Notation D t DD t D t DD t – Slow

Track 5 Arat Akhu Net

This song is based on a poem put together based on various scriptures related to the goddess which extol her attributes and divine qualities. Composed in the traditional ritual style, this song contains echoes of the ancient and modern vocal traditions of the middle east and Ancient Egypt.

Arat Net   (Goddess Net)
Akhu Asha   (her glories are many)
Neterit aah   (she is the great goddess)
Nt Sefech Cheras Senhu-s (Her vail is not revealed)

Arat Net   (Goddess Net)
Mehenit ta-pet   (she is the weaver of the world and the heavens)
Arat Net   (Goddess Net)
Chemam neteru   (she is the creator of the gods and goddesses)

Arat Net   (Goddess Net)
Mehurt mesu Ra   (she is the divine cow that gave birth to Ra)
Arat Net   (Goddess Net)
Nt Rekh s Shetat sen (not known is she, she is hidden)

Drumming Notation Basic Slow – DD tk DD tk
Advanced Slow – DDDDD t t t DDDDD t t t

101

Track 6 Net Net Dua Net Long Version (See track #2)

Vocals: Sebai Maa and Karen "Dja" Ashby (on track 2), keyboard: Sebai Maa, Sistrums: Sebai Maa, Cymbals: Sebai Maa, Nefer: Sebai Maa, Clapping: Sebai Maa, Tar: Sebai Maa. Featuring the piano playing of Reginald Ashby Sr. (On track 4)

Hekau - Words of Power - Chanting Guide

Hekau	# of recitations per minute			# per hour		
	Low	Med	High	Low	Med	High
Om	140	250	400	8400	15000	24000
Om Asar Aset Heru	80	120	140	4800	7200	9000
Dua Ra, Dua Ra, Dua Ra Khepera	70	110	130	4200	6600	7800
amma su en pa neter sauu - k su emment en pa neter au duanu ma qedi pa	6	8	10	360	480	600
Dua Asar Unefer Neteraah Dua Asar Her Abdu Dua Asar Neb Djeta Dua Asar Suten Heh!	6	8	10	360	480	600
42 Precepts of				2	4	6
Hymns of Amun				2	4	6
Any of the daily recitation Collections (morning, noontime or evening)				1	2	3

Kemetic Hieroglyphs of the
Chant and Divine Singing Tradition

or

Uash (Ushet)- praise worship

Uashu - praises, words of worship

S-uash - to praise to worship

 Shmai- make music

 Shmai- sing

Shmait - female musician singer

Shmaiti - male musician singer

Hesi -Chant, sing repeatedly praises

Dua - praises, adorations
to the divine (standing or sitting)

Dua Neter - title of the priestess of Amun

Dua Neter - title of the priestess of Amun

Smai Tawi - Egyptian Yoga

Visit the virtual temple online at www.Semauniversity.org and join in with the worship program. See the candle, incense, libation and offerings and hear the Medu Neter chants.

NOTES

---

[1] Generally referred to as chapter 125-

[2] Appendices are provided to show an expanded meaning of the utterances. They are taken from the same numbered utterances contained in different papyri.

[3] Pa Neter-The Supreme Being from whom emanate the gods and goddesses. The goal of the Pert M Heru is to lead a person to an ultimate encounter to face God and become one with {her/him}.

[4] Translation from the original text by Dr. Muata Ashby

[5] Bragging, pretentious, arrogant, egoistic.

[6] Selfishness.

[7] Generally referred to as chapter 175.

[8] This chapter is an evolution of Utterances that are found in the *Pyramid Texts* and the *Coffin Texts* which relate to Atum as the first primordial being. It is an instructional dialogue much in the Vedantic tradition of India wherein the god or goddess {him/her} self speaks to the spiritual aspirant directly. This chapter thereby shows that the later versions of the *Prt m Hru* incorporate and evolved the teachings of the earlier versions, since this form of dialogue is not found in the earlier versions.

[9] Nut is the goddess of the sky or heaven. Since all planets are as if given birth by the heavens, it follows that all things on earth, including plants, animals and human beings, are children of Nut. Also, Nut is the mother of the gods and goddesses: Asar, Aset, Set and Nebethet, and by association also, their progeny: Heru and Anpu. The conflict being alluded to here is he one between Asar and Set, and Set and Heru. See the book *The Ausarian Resurrection* by Muata Ashby. This question is very similar to one which occurs in the Bhagavad Gita of India where the question is asked: *Gita: Chapter Arjuna Vishad Yogah--The Yoga of Arjuna's Dejection* 1. Dhritarashtra asked: O Sanjaya, what did my sons and the sons of (my brother) Pandu (the Pandavas) do, assembled in the holy place of Kurukshetra, eager to fight?

[10] These specific infractions are mentioned in the Hermetic texts-See the book *The Ausarian Resurrection* by Muata Ashby.

[11] Maat Philosophy holds that leading a life of unrighteousness renders a human being spiritually weak and susceptible to temptations of the lower nature. See the book *Wisdom of Maati* by Muata Ashby.

[12] The secret nature of the offences against the Divine (Djehuti) relate to the sins committed by people of which only god is aware. While there may be no human witnesses, Djehuti, who symbolizes the cosmic intellect, is always aware of the acts of every personality.

[13] A tool used for printing or gilding letters on book bindings. This is a humble invitation to the Higher Self to be the guiding force in one's life as opposed to the ego and its unrighteousness that was referred to earlier. This verse points to the understanding that one must be not only free from committing unrighteousness, but also there must be righteousness in the heart as well (internal, mental righteousness). Here the initiate is to quash all egoistic notions and place {him/her} in the hands of God. A similar teaching occurs in Indian mysticism as the spiritual aspirant is asked to allow {him/her} to become the flute upon which God, in the form of Krishna, plays the divine melody of prosperity and spiritual salvation. This means giving oneself to God, the ultimate devotional gesture in any religion.

[14] The place refers to the Netherworld, the afterlife state.

[15] Glorious spirit status, i.e. spiritual enlightenment.

[16] The place of duality and consumption, i.e. human existence on earth.

[17] This passage relates to the dissolution of creation back into the primordial state, from the Nun, or primeval waters from which all things emerged in the beginning. This is an important teaching which shows that Ancient Egyptian mythology and philosophy recognized the concept that creation

is not a linear event, having a beginning and an end, but it is akin to a cycle which recurs at given intervals, governed by Divinity.

[18] Royal standard. This symbol was used in ancient times prior to the cartouche for inscribing royal names.

[19] Heru underwent a struggle with Set over the rulership of Egypt. This is symbolic of the struggle of the spiritual aspirant with {his/her} lower self. When Heru is established, it means a spiritual victory, Maak-heru-Spiritual Enlightenment.

[20] Spiritual Enlightenment.

21 THE TERMS "HARI" AND "OM" IN ANCIENT EGYPT AND INDIA

While *Om* is most commonly known as a *Sanskrit* mantra (word of power from India), it also appears in the Ancient Egyptian texts and is closely related to the Kamitan *Amun* in sound and Amen of Christianity. More importantly, it has the same meaning as Amun and is therefore completely compatible with the energy pattern of the entire group. According to the Egyptian Leyden papyrus, the name of the "Hidden God," referring to Amun, may be pronounced as *Om*, or *Am*.

Below you will find the ancient glyphs of the ancient Egyptian OM symbol. Note the similarity to the Indian symbol that follows.

"OM" from the Ancient Egyptian Leyden Papyrus

The ancient African text containing the OM is found in the Leyden Magical Papyrus in which Supreme Being is described as follows:

> "Great is thy name, Heir is thy name, Excellent is thy name, Hidden is thy name,. Mighty one of the gods and goddesses is thy name, "He whose name is hidden from all the gods and goddesses is thy name, OM (☺✅), Mighty Am is thy name; All the gods and goddesses is thy name…"

We know that OM is the name of Amun because of the epithet "Hidden" and OM is the nameless Ancient divinity because of the epithet "name is hidden". OM is also the ancient divinity Neberdjer (All encompassing Divinity) because of the epithet "All the gods and goddesses" so OM is the name given to the most ancient divinities of Kamit (Egypt) dating to the predynastic era (prior to 5000 BCE).

Om is a powerful sound; it represents the primordial sound of creation. Thus it appears in Ancient Egypt as Om or Am, in modern day India as Om, and in Christianity as Amen, being derived from Amun. Om may also be used for engendering mental calm prior to beginning recitation of a longer set of words of power or it may be used alone as described above. One Indian Tantric scripture (*Tattva Prakash*) states that Om or AUM can be used to achieve the mental state free of physical identification and can bring union with *Brahman* (the Absolute transcendental Supreme Being - God) if it is repeated 300,000 times. In this sense, mantras such as Om, Soham, Sivoham, Aham Brahmasmi are called *Moksha Mantras* or mantras which lead to union with the Absolute Self.

Their shortness promotes greater concentration and force toward the primordial level of consciousness.

The Indian Sanskrit Symbol "Aum" or "Om"

There is one more important divine name which is common to both Indian as well as Ancient Egyptian mystical philosophy. The Sanskrit mantra *Hari Om* is composed of Om preceded by the word Hari. In Hinduism, *Hari* means: "He who is Tawny." The definition of tawny is: "A light golden brown." However, Vishnu is oftentimes represented as "blue-black." This is a reference to the dark colored skin of Vishnu and Krishna. Vishnu is usually depicted with a deep blue and Krishna is depicted with a deep blue or black hue symbolizing infinity and transcendence. Hari is one of Krishna's or Vishnu's many divine names.

The Ancient Egyptian Word "Haari"

In the Ancient Egyptian mystical texts used to promote spiritual development (Words of Power or Heka - mantras), the word Haari also appears as one of the divine names[21] of God. Thus, the hekau-mantra Hari Om was also known and used in Ancient Egypt and constitutes a most powerful formula for mystical spiritual practice. Om or Am in Ancient Egypt was a shortened version of Amun, the divinity who like Vishnu and Krishna is depicted in Black or Blue (tawny). "Amun" also means hidden consciousness.

Amun (Hidden essence of creation-witnessing consciousness)

SEMA INSTITUTE

Cruzian Mystic P.O.Box 570459, Miami, Florida. 33257 (305) 378-6253, Fax. (305) 378-6253

www.Egyptianyoga.com

OTHER BOOKS FROM C M BOOKS

**P.O.Box 570459
Miami, Florida, 33257
(305) 378-6253 Fax: (305) 378-6253**

This book is part of a series on the study and practice of Ancient Egyptian Yoga and Mystical Spirituality based on the writings of Dr. Muata Abhaya Ashby. They are also part of the Egyptian Yoga Course provided by the Sema Institute of Yoga. Below you will find a listing of the other books in this series. For more information send for the Egyptian Yoga Book-Audio-Video Catalog or the Egyptian Yoga Course Catalog.

Now you can study the teachings of Egyptian and Indian Yoga wisdom and Spirituality with the Egyptian Yoga Mystical Spirituality Series. The Egyptian Yoga Series takes you through the Initiation process and lead you to understand the mysteries of the soul and the Divine and to attain the highest goal of life: ENLIGHTENMENT. The *Egyptian Yoga Series*, takes you on an in depth study of Ancient Egyptian mythology and their inner mystical meaning. Each Book is prepared for the serious student of the mystical sciences and provides a study of the teachings along with exercises, assignments and projects to make the teachings understood and effective in real life. The Series is part of the Egyptian Yoga course but may be purchased even if you are not taking the course. The series is ideal for study groups.

Prices subject to change.

1. EGYPTIAN YOGA: THE PHILOSOPHY OF ENLIGHTENMENT An original, fully illustrated work, including hieroglyphs, detailing the meaning of the Egyptian mysteries, tantric yoga, psycho-spiritual and physical exercises. Egyptian Yoga is a guide to the practice of the highest spiritual philosophy

which leads to absolute freedom from human misery and to immortality. It is well known by scholars that Egyptian philosophy is the basis of Western and Middle Eastern religious philosophies such as *Christianity, Islam, Judaism,* the *Kabala,* and Greek philosophy, but what about Indian philosophy, Yoga and Taoism? What were the original teachings? How can they be practiced today? What is the source of pain and suffering in the world and what is the solution? Discover the deepest mysteries of the mind and universe within and outside of your self. 8.5" X 11" ISBN: 1-884564-01-1 Soft $19.95

2.   EGYPTIAN YOGA: African Religion Volume 2- Theban Theology U.S. In this long awaited sequel to *Egyptian Yoga: The Philosophy of Enlightenment* you will take a fascinating and enlightening journey back in time and discover the teachings which constituted the epitome of Ancient Egyptian spiritual wisdom. What are the disciplines which lead to the fulfillment of all desires? Delve into the three states of consciousness (waking, dream and deep sleep) and the fourth state which transcends them all, Neberdjer, "The Absolute." These teachings of the city of Waset (Thebes) were the crowning achievement of the Sages of Ancient Egypt. They establish the standard mystical keys for understanding the profound mystical symbolism of the Triad of human consciousness. ISBN 1-884564-39-9 $23.95

3.   THE KEMETIC DIET: GUIDE TO HEALTH, DIET AND FASTING Health issues have always been important to human beings since the beginning of time. The earliest records of history show that the art of healing was held in high esteem since the time of Ancient Egypt. In the early 20th century, medical doctors had almost attained the status of sainthood by the promotion of the idea that they alone were "scientists" while other healing modalities and traditional healers who did not follow the "scientific method' were nothing but superstitious, ignorant charlatans who at best would take the money of their clients and at worst kill them with the unscientific "snake oils" and "irrational theories". In the late 20th century, the failure of the modern medical establishment's ability to lead the general public to good health, promoted the move by many in society towards "alternative medicine". Alternative medicine disciplines are those healing modalities which do not adhere to the philosophy of allopathic medicine. Allopathic medicine is what medical doctors practice by an large. It is the theory that disease is caused by agencies outside the body such as bacteria, viruses or physical means which affect the body. These can therefore be treated by medicines and therapies The natural healing method began in the absence of extensive technologies with the idea that all the answers for health may be found in nature or rather, the deviation from nature. Therefore, the health of the body can be restored by correcting the aberration and thereby restoring balance. This is the area that will be covered in this volume. Allopathic techniques have their place in the art of healing. However, we should not forget that the body is a grand achievement of the spirit and built into it is the capacity to maintain itself and heal itself. Ashby, Muata ISBN: 1-884564-49-6 $28.95

4. INITIATION INTO EGYPTIAN YOGA Shedy: Spiritual discipline or program, to go deeply into the mysteries, to study the mystery teachings and literature profoundly, to penetrate the mysteries. You will learn about the mysteries of initiation into the teachings and practice of Yoga and how to become an Initiate of the mystical sciences. This insightful manual is the first in a series which introduces you to the goals of daily spiritual and yoga practices: Meditation, Diet, Words of Power and the ancient wisdom teachings. 8.5" X 11" ISBN 1-884564-02-X Soft Cover $24.95 U.S.

5. *THE AFRICAN ORIGINS OF CIVILIZATION, RELIGION AND YOGA SPIRITUALITY AND ETHICS PHILOSOPHY* HARD COVER EDITION Part 1, Part 2, Part 3 in one volume 683 Pages Hard Cover First Edition Three volumes in one. Over the past several years I have been asked to put together in one volume the most important evidences showing the correlations and common teachings between Kamitan (Ancient Egyptian) culture and religion and that of India. The questions of the history of Ancient Egypt, and the latest archeological evidences showing civilization and culture in Ancient Egypt and its spread to other countries, has intrigued many scholars as well as mystics over the years. Also, the possibility that Ancient Egyptian Priests and Priestesses migrated to Greece, India and other countries to carry on the traditions of the Ancient Egyptian Mysteries, has been speculated over the years as well. In chapter 1 of the book *Egyptian Yoga The Philosophy of Enlightenment,* 1995, I first introduced the deepest comparison between Ancient Egypt and India that had been brought forth up to that time. Now, in the year 2001 this new book, *THE AFRICAN ORIGINS OF CIVILIZATION, MYSTICAL RELIGION AND YOGA PHILOSOPHY,* more fully explores the motifs, symbols and philosophical correlations between Ancient Egyptian and Indian mysticism and clearly shows not only that Ancient Egypt and India were connected culturally but also spiritually. How does this knowledge help the spiritual aspirant? This discovery has great importance for the Yogis and mystics who follow the philosophy of Ancient Egypt and the mysticism of India. It means that India has a longer history and heritage than was previously understood. It shows that the mysteries of Ancient Egypt were essentially a yoga tradition which did not die but rather developed into the modern day systems of Yoga technology of India. It further shows that African culture developed Yoga Mysticism earlier than any other civilization in history. All of this expands our understanding of the unity of culture and the deep legacy of Yoga, which stretches into the distant past, beyond the Indus Valley civilization, the earliest known high culture in India as well as the Vedic tradition of Aryan culture. Therefore, Yoga culture and mysticism is the oldest known tradition of spiritual development and Indian mysticism is an extension of the Ancient Egyptian mysticism. By understanding the legacy which Ancient Egypt gave to India the mysticism of India is better understood and by comprehending the heritage of Indian Yoga, which is rooted in Ancient Egypt the Mysticism of Ancient Egypt is also better understood. This expanded understanding allows us to prove the underlying kinship of humanity,

111

through the common symbols, motifs and philosophies which are not disparate and confusing teachings but in reality expressions of the same study of truth through metaphysics and mystical realization of Self. (HARD COVER) ISBN: 1-884564-50-X $45.00 U.S.   81/2" X 11"

6.   AFRICAN ORIGINS BOOK 1 PART 1 African Origins of African Civilization, Religion, Yoga Mysticism and Ethics Philosophy-Soft Cover $24.95 ISBN: 1-884564-55-0

7.   AFRICAN ORIGINS BOOK 2 PART 2 African Origins of Western Civilization, Religion and Philosophy (Soft) -Soft Cover $24.95 ISBN: 1-884564-56-9

8.   EGYPT AND INDIA AFRICAN ORIGINS OF Eastern Civilization, Religion, Yoga Mysticism and Philosophy-Soft Cover $29.95 (Soft) ISBN: 1-884564-57-7

9.   THE MYSTERIES OF ISIS: **The Ancient Egyptian Philosophy of Self-Realization** - There are several paths to discover the Divine and the mysteries of the higher Self. This volume details the mystery teachings of the goddess Aset (Isis) from Ancient Egypt- the path of wisdom. It includes the teachings of her temple and the disciplines that are enjoined for the initiates of the temple of Aset as they were given in ancient times. Also, this book includes the teachings of the main myths of Aset that lead a human being to spiritual enlightenment and immortality. Through the study of ancient myth and the illumination of initiatic understanding the idea of God is expanded from the mythological comprehension to the metaphysical. Then this metaphysical understanding is related to you, the student, so as to begin understanding your true divine nature. ISBN 1-884564-24-0 $22.99

10.   EGYPTIAN PROVERBS: collection of —Ancient Egyptian Proverbs and Wisdom Teachings -How to live according to MAAT Philosophy. Beginning Meditation. All proverbs are indexed for easy searches. For the first time in one volume, ——Ancient Egyptian Proverbs, wisdom teachings and meditations, fully illustrated with hieroglyphic text and symbols. EGYPTIAN PROVERBS is a unique collection of knowledge and wisdom which you can put into practice today and transform your life. $14.95 U.S   ISBN: 1-884564-00-3

11.   GOD OF LOVE: THE PATH OF DIVINE LOVE The Process of Mystical Transformation and The Path of Divine Love   This Volume focuses on the ancient wisdom teachings of "Neter Merri" –the Ancient Egyptian philosophy of Divine Love and how to use them in a scientific process for self-transformation. Love is one of the most powerful human emotions. It is also the source of Divine feeling that unifies God and the individual human being. When love is fragmented and diminished by egoism the Divine connection is lost. The Ancient tradition of Neter Merri leads human beings back to their Divine connection, allowing them to discover their innate glorious self that is actually

Divine and immortal. This volume will detail the process of transformation from ordinary consciousness to cosmic consciousness through the integrated practice of the teachings and the path of Devotional Love toward the Divine. 5.5"x 8.5" ISBN 1-884564-11-9 $22.95

12. INTRODUCTION TO MAAT PHILOSOPHY: Spiritual Enlightenment Through the Path of Virtue   Known as Karma Yoga in India, the teachings of MAAT for living virtuously and with orderly wisdom are explained and the student is to begin practicing the precepts of Maat in daily life so as to promote the process of purification of the heart in preparation for the judgment of the soul. This judgment will be understood not as an event that will occur at the time of death but as an event that occurs continuously, at every moment in the life of the individual. The student will learn how to become allied with the forces of the Higher Self and to thereby begin cleansing the mind (heart) of impurities so as to attain a higher vision of reality. ISBN 1-884564-20-8 $22.99

13. MEDITATION The Ancient Egyptian Path to Enlightenment   Many people do not know about the rich history of meditation practice in Ancient Egypt. This volume outlines the theory of meditation and presents the Ancient Egyptian Hieroglyphic text which give instruction as to the nature of the mind and its three modes of expression. It also presents the texts which give instruction on the practice of meditation for spiritual Enlightenment and unity with the Divine. This volume allows the reader to begin practicing meditation by explaining, in easy to understand terms, the simplest form of meditation and working up to the most advanced form which was practiced in ancient times and which is still practiced by yogis around the world in modern times. ISBN 1-884564-27-7 $22.99

14. THE GLORIOUS LIGHT MEDITATION TECHNIQUE OF ANCIENT EGYPT New for the year 2000. This volume is based on the earliest known instruction in history given for the practice of formal meditation. Discovered by Dr. Muata Ashby, it is inscribed on the walls of the Tomb of Seti I in Thebes Egypt. This volume details the philosophy and practice of this unique system of meditation originated in Ancient Egypt and the earliest practice of meditation known in the world which occurred in the most advanced African Culture. ISBN: 1-884564-15-1 $16.95 (PB)

15. THE SERPENT POWER: The Ancient Egyptian Mystical Wisdom of the Inner Life Force.   This Volume specifically deals with the latent life Force energy of the universe and in the human body, its control and sublimation. How to develop the Life Force energy of the subtle body. This Volume will introduce the esoteric wisdom of the science of how virtuous living acts in a subtle and mysterious way to cleanse the latent psychic energy conduits and vortices of the spiritual body. ISBN 1-884564-19-4 $22.95

16.   EGYPTIAN YOGA *The Postures of The Gods and Goddesses* Discover the physical postures and exercises practiced thousands of years ago in Ancient Egypt which are today known as Yoga exercises. Discover the history of the postures and how they were transferred from Ancient Egypt in Africa to India through Buddhist Tantrism. Then practice the postures as you discover the mythic teaching that originally gave birth to the postures and was practiced by the Ancient Egyptian priests and priestesses. This work is based on the pictures and teachings from the Creation story of Ra, The Asarian Resurrection Myth and the carvings and reliefs from various Temples in Ancient Egypt 8.5" X 11" ISBN 1-884564-10-0 Soft Cover $21.95   Exercise video $20

17.   SACRED SEXUALITY: EGYPTIAN TANTRA YOGA: The Art of Sex Sublimation and Universal Consciousness This Volume will expand on the male and female principles within the human body and in the universe and further detail the sublimation of sexual energy into spiritual energy. The student will study the deities Min and Hathor, Asar and Aset, Geb and Nut and discover the mystical implications for a practical spiritual discipline. This Volume will also focus on the Tantric aspects of Ancient Egyptian and Indian mysticism, the purpose of sex and the mystical teachings of sexual sublimation which lead to self-knowledge and Enlightenment.   5.5"x 8.5"   ISBN 1-884564-03-8 $24.95

18.   AFRICAN RELIGION Volume 4: ASARIAN THEOLOGY: RESURRECTING OSIRIS The path of Mystical Awakening and the Keys to Immortality NEW REVISED AND EXPANDED EDITION!   The Ancient Sages created stories based on human and superhuman beings whose struggles, aspirations, needs and desires ultimately lead them to discover their true Self. The myth of Aset, Asar and Heru is no exception in this area. While there is no one source where the entire story may be found, pieces of it are inscribed in various ancient Temples walls, tombs, steles and papyri. For the first time available, the complete myth of Asar, Aset and Heru has been compiled from original Ancient Egyptian, Greek and Coptic Texts. This epic myth has been richly illustrated with reliefs from the Temple of Heru at Edfu, the Temple of Aset at Philae, the Temple of Asar at Abydos, the Temple of Hathor at Denderah and various papyri, inscriptions and reliefs.   Discover the myth which inspired the teachings of the *Shetaut Neter* (Egyptian Mystery System - Egyptian Yoga) and the Egyptian Book of Coming Forth By Day. Also, discover the three levels of Ancient Egyptian Religion, how to understand the mysteries of the Duat or Astral World and how to discover the abode of the Supreme in the Amenta, *The Other World* The ancient religion of Asar, Aset and Heru, if properly understood, contains all of the elements necessary to lead the sincere aspirant to attain immortality through inner self-discovery. This volume presents the entire myth and explores the main mystical themes and rituals associated with the myth for understating human existence, creation and the way to achieve spiritual emancipation - *Resurrection.* The Asarian myth is so powerful that it influenced and is still having an effect on the major world religions. Discover the origins and mystical

meaning of the Christian Trinity, the Eucharist ritual and the ancient origin of the birthday of Jesus Christ. Soft Cover ISBN: 1-884564-27-5 $24.95

19. THE EGYPTIAN BOOK OF THE DEAD MYSTICISM OF THE PERT EM HERU " I Know myself, I know myself, I am One With God!–From the Pert Em Heru "The Ru Pert em Heru" or "Ancient Egyptian Book of The Dead," or "Book of Coming Forth By Day" as it is more popularly known, has fascinated the world since the successful translation of Ancient Egyptian hieroglyphic scripture over 150 years ago. The astonishing writings in it reveal that the Ancient Egyptians believed in life after death and in an ultimate destiny to discover the Divine. The elegance and aesthetic beauty of the hieroglyphic text itself has inspired many see it as an art form in and of itself. But is there more to it than that? Did the Ancient Egyptian wisdom contain more than just aphorisms and hopes of eternal life beyond death? In this volume Dr. Muata Ashby, the author of over 25 books on Ancient Egyptian Yoga Philosophy has produced a new translation of the original texts which uncovers a mystical teaching underlying the sayings and rituals instituted by the Ancient Egyptian Sages and Saints. "Once the philosophy of Ancient Egypt is understood as a mystical tradition instead of as a religion or primitive mythology, it reveals its secrets which if practiced today will lead anyone to discover the glory of spiritual self-discovery. The Pert em Heru is in every way comparable to the Indian Upanishads or the Tibetan Book of the Dead." $28.95   ISBN# 1-884564-28-3 Size: 8½" X 11

20. African Religion VOL. 1- ANUNIAN THEOLOGY THE MYSTERIES OF RA The Philosophy of Anu and The Mystical Teachings of The Ancient Egyptian Creation Myth Discover the mystical teachings contained in the Creation Myth and the gods and goddesses who brought creation and human beings into existence. The Creation myth of Anu is the source of Anunian Theology but also of the other main theological systems of Ancient Egypt that also influenced other world religions including Christianity, Hinduism and Buddhism. The Creation Myth holds the key to understanding the universe and for attaining spiritual Enlightenment. ISBN: 1-884564-38-0 $19.95

21. African Religion VOL 3: Memphite Theology: MYSTERIES OF MIND Mystical Psychology & Mental Health for Enlightenment and Immortality based on the Ancient Egyptian Philosophy of Menefer -Mysticism of Ptah, Egyptian Physics and Yoga Metaphysics and the Hidden properties of Matter. This volume uncovers the mystical psychology of the Ancient Egyptian wisdom teachings centering on the philosophy of the Ancient Egyptian city of Menefer (Memphite Theology). How to understand the mind and how to control the senses and lead the mind to health, clarity and mystical self-discovery. This Volume will also go deeper into the philosophy of God as creation and will explore the concepts of modern science and how they correlate with ancient teachings. This Volume will lay the ground work for the understanding of the

philosophy of universal consciousness and the initiatic/yogic insight into who or what is God? ISBN 1-884564-07-0 $22.95

22.   AFRICAN RELIGION VOLUME 5: THE GODDESS AND THE EGYPTIAN MYSTERIESTHE PATH OF THE GODDESS THE GODDESS PATH The Secret Forms of the Goddess and the Rituals of Resurrection The Supreme Being may be worshipped as father or as mother. *Ushet Rekhat* or *Mother Worship*, is the spiritual process of worshipping the Divine in the form of the Divine Goddess. It celebrates the most important forms of the Goddess including *Nathor, Maat, Aset, Arat, Amentet and Hathor* and explores their mystical meaning as well as the rising of *Sirius,* the star of Aset (Aset) and the new birth of Hor (Heru). The end of the year is a time of reckoning, reflection and engendering a new or renewed positive movement toward attaining spiritual Enlightenment. The Mother Worship devotional meditation ritual, performed on five days during the month of December and on New Year's Eve, is based on the Ushet Rekhit. During the ceremony, the cosmic forces, symbolized by Sirius - and the constellation of Orion ---, are harnessed through the understanding and devotional attitude of the participant. This propitiation draws the light of wisdom and health to all those who share in the ritual, leading to prosperity and wisdom. $14.95 ISBN 1-884564-18-6

23.   *THE MYSTICAL JOURNEY FROM JESUS TO CHRIST* Discover the ancient Egyptian origins of Christianity before the Catholic Church and learn the mystical teachings given by Jesus to assist all humanity in becoming Christlike. Discover the secret meaning of the Gospels that were discovered in Egypt. Also discover how and why so many Christian churches came into being. Discover that the Bible still holds the keys to mystical realization even though its original writings were changed by the church. Discover how to practice the original teachings of Christianity which leads to the Kingdom of Heaven. $24.95 ISBN# 1-884564-05-4 size: 8½" X 11"

24.   THE STORY OF ASAR, ASET AND HERU: An Ancient Egyptian Legend (For Children)   Now for the first time, the most ancient myth of Ancient Egypt comes alive for children. Inspired by the books *The Asarian Resurrection: The Ancient Egyptian Bible* and *The Mystical Teachings of The Asarian Resurrection, The Story of Asar, Aset and Heru* is an easy to understand and thrilling tale which inspired the children of Ancient Egypt to aspire to greatness and righteousness.   If you and your child have enjoyed stories like *The Lion King* and *Star Wars you will love The Story of Asar, Aset and Heru.* Also, if you know the story of Jesus and Krishna you will discover than Ancient Egypt had a similar myth and that this myth carries important spiritual teachings for living a fruitful and fulfilling life.   This book may be used along with *The Parents Guide To The Asarian Resurrection Myth: How to Teach Yourself and Your Child the Principles of Universal Mystical Religion.* The guide provides some background to the Asarian Resurrection myth and it also gives insight into the mystical teachings contained in it which you may introduce to your child. It is designed

116

for parents who wish to grow spiritually with their children and it serves as an introduction for those who would like to study the Asarian Resurrection Myth in depth and to practice its teachings. 8.5" X 11"   ISBN: 1-884564-31-3 $12.95

25.   THE PARENTS GUIDE TO THE AUSARIAN RESURRECTION MYTH: How to Teach Yourself and Your Child the Principles of Universal Mystical Religion.   This insightful manual brings for the timeless wisdom of the ancient through the Ancient Egyptian myth of Asar, Aset and Heru and the mystical teachings contained in it for parents who want to guide their children to understand and practice the teachings of mystical spirituality. This manual may be used with the children's storybook *The Story of Asar, Aset and Heru* by Dr. Muata Abhaya Ashby.   ISBN: 1-884564-30-5 $16.95

26.   HEALING THE CRIMINAL HEART. Introduction to Maat Philosophy, Yoga and Spiritual Redemption Through the Path of Virtue   Who is a criminal? Is there such a thing as a criminal heart? What is the source of evil and sinfulness and is there any way to rise above it? Is there redemption for those who have committed sins, even the worst crimes?   Ancient Egyptian mystical psychology holds important answers to these questions. Over ten thousand years ago mystical psychologists, the Sages of Ancient Egypt, studied and charted the human mind and spirit and laid out a path which will lead to spiritual redemption, prosperity and Enlightenment.   This introductory volume brings forth the teachings of the Asarian Resurrection, the most important myth of Ancient Egypt, with relation to the faults of human existence: anger, hatred, greed, lust, animosity, discontent, ignorance, egoism jealousy, bitterness, and a myriad of psycho-spiritual ailments which keep a human being in a state of negativity and adversity   ISBN: 1-884564-17-8 $15.95

27.   TEMPLE RITUAL OF THE ANCIENT EGYPTIAN MYSTERIES-- THEATER & DRAMA OF THE ANCIENT EGYPTIAN MYSTERIES: Details the practice of the mysteries and ritual program of the temple and the philosophy an practice of the ritual of the mysteries, its purpose and execution. Featuring the Ancient Egyptian stage play-"The Enlightenment of Hathor' Based on an Ancient Egyptian Drama, The original Theater -Mysticism of the Temple of Hetheru 1-884564-14-3 $19.95   By Dr. Muata Ashby

28.   GUIDE TO PRINT ON DEMAND: SELF-PUBLISH FOR PROFIT, SPIRITUAL FULFILLMENT AND SERVICE TO HUMANITY Everyone asks us how we produced so many books in such a short time. Here are the secrets to writing and producing books that uplift humanity and how to get them printed for a fraction of the regular cost. Anyone can become an author even if they have limited funds. All that is necessary is the willingness to learn how the printing and book business work and the desire to follow the special instructions given here for preparing your manuscript format. Then you take your work directly to the non-

traditional companies who can produce your books for less than the traditional book printer can. ISBN: 1-884564-40-2 $16.95 U. S.

29.   Egyptian Mysteries: Vol. 1, Shetaut Neter What are the Mysteries? For thousands of years the spiritual tradition of Ancient Egypt, S*hetaut Neter, "*The Egyptian Mysteries," "The Secret Teachings," have fascinated, tantalized and amazed the world. At one time exalted and recognized as the highest culture of the world, by Africans, Europeans, Asiatics, Hindus, Buddhists and other cultures of the ancient world, in time it was shunned by the emerging orthodox world religions. Its temples desecrated, its philosophy maligned, its tradition spurned, its philosophy dormant in the mystical *Medu Neter*, the mysterious hieroglyphic texts which hold the secret symbolic meaning that has scarcely been discerned up to now. What are the secrets of *Nehast* {spiritual awakening and emancipation, resurrection}. More than just a literal translation, this volume is for awakening to the secret code *Shetitu* of the teaching which was not deciphered by Egyptologists, nor could be understood by ordinary spiritualists. This book is a reinstatement of the original science made available for our times, to the reincarnated followers of Ancient Egyptian culture and the prospect of spiritual freedom to break the bonds of *Khemn*, "ignorance," and slavery to evil forces: *Såaa* . ISBN: 1-884564-41-0 $19.99

30.   EGYPTIAN MYSTERIES VOL 2: Dictionary of Gods and Goddesses This book is about the mystery of neteru, the gods and goddesses of Ancient Egypt (Kamit, Kemet). Neteru means "Gods and Goddesses." But the Neterian teaching of Neteru represents more than the usual limited modern day concept of "divinities" or "spirits." The Neteru of Kamit are also metaphors, cosmic principles and vehicles for the enlightening teachings of Shetaut Neter (Ancient Egyptian-African Religion). Actually they are the elements for one of the most advanced systems of spirituality ever conceived in human history. Understanding the concept of neteru provides a firm basis for spiritual evolution and the pathway for viable culture, peace on earth and a healthy human society. Why is it important to have gods and goddesses in our lives? In order for spiritual evolution to be possible, once a human being has accepted that there is existence after death and there is a transcendental being who exists beyond time and space knowledge, human beings need a connection to that which transcends the ordinary experience of human life in time and space and a means to understand the transcendental reality beyond the mundane reality. ISBN: 1-884564-23-2 $21.95

31.   EGYPTIAN MYSTERIES VOL. 3 The Priests and Priestesses of Ancient Egypt This volume details the path of Neterian priesthood, the joys, challenges and rewards of advanced Neterian life, the teachings that allowed the priests and priestesses to manage the most long lived civilization in human history and how that path can be adopted today; for those who want to tread the path of the Clergy of Shetaut Neter. ISBN: 1-884564-53-4 $24.95

32. The War of Heru and Set: The Struggle of Good and Evil for Control of the World and The Human Soul This volume contains a novelized version of the Asarian Resurrection myth that is based on the actual scriptures presented in the Book Asarian Religion (old name –Resurrecting Osiris). This volume is prepared in the form of a screenplay and can be easily adapted to be used as a stage play. Spiritual seeking is a mythic journey that has many emotional highs and lows, ecstasies and depressions, victories and frustrations. This is the War of Life that is played out in the myth as the struggle of Heru and Set and those are mythic characters that represent the human Higher and Lower self. How to understand the war and emerge victorious in the journey o life? The ultimate victory and fulfillment can be experienced, which is not changeable or lost in time. The purpose of myth is to convey the wisdom of life through the story of divinities who show the way to overcome the challenges and foibles of life. In this volume the feelings and emotions of the characters of the myth have been highlighted to show the deeply rich texture of the Ancient Egyptian myth. This myth contains deep spiritual teachings and insights into the nature of self, of God and the mysteries of life and the means to discover the true meaning of life and thereby achieve the true purpose of life. To become victorious in the battle of life means to become the King (or Queen) of Egypt.Have you seen movies like The Lion King, Hamlet, The Odyssey, or The Little Buddha? These have been some of the most popular movies in modern times. The Sema Institute of Yoga is dedicated to researching and presenting the wisdom and culture of ancient Africa. The Script is designed to be produced as a motion picture but may be addapted for the theater as well. $21.95 copyright 1998 By Dr. Muata Ashby ISBN 1-8840564-44-5

33. AFRICAN DIONYSUS: FROM EGYPT TO GREECE: The Kamitan Origins of Greek Culture and Religion ISBN: 1-884564-47-X FROM EGYPT TO GREECE This insightful manual is a reference to Ancient Egyptian mythology and philosophy and its correlation to what later became known as Greek and Rome mythology and philosophy. It outlines the basic tenets of the mythologies and shoes the ancient origins of Greek culture in Ancient Egypt. This volume also documents the origins of the Greek alphabet in Egypt as well as Greek religion, myth and philosophy of the gods and goddesses from Egypt from the myth of Atlantis and archaic period with the Minoans to the Classical period. This volume also acts as a resource for Colleges students who would like to set up fraternities and sororities based on the original Ancient Egyptian principles of Sheti and Maat philosophy. ISBN: 1-884564-47-X $22.95 U.S.

34. THE FORTY TWO PRECEPTS OF MAAT, THE PHILOSOPHY OF RIGHTEOUS ACTION AND THE ANCIENT EGYPTIAN WISDOM TEXTS ADVANCED STUDIES This manual is designed for use with the 1998 Maat Philosophy Class conducted by Dr. Muata Ashby. This is a detailed study of Maat Philosophy. It contains a compilation of the 42 laws or precepts of Maat and the corresponding principles which they represent along with the teachings

of the ancient Egyptian Sages relating to each. Maat philosophy was the basis of Ancient Egyptian society and government as well as the heart of Ancient Egyptian myth and spirituality. Maat is at once a goddess, a cosmic force and a living social doctrine, which promotes social harmony and thereby paves the way for spiritual evolution in all levels of society. ISBN: 1-884564-48-8 $16.95 U.S.

35. **THE SECRET LOTUS:** *Poetry of Enlightenment*Discover the mystical sentiment of the Kemetic teaching as expressed through the poetry of Sebai Muata Ashby. The teaching of spiritual awakening is uniquely experienced when the poetic sensibility is present. This first volume contains the poems written between 1996 and 2003. **1-884564--16 -X $16.99**

36. **Ancient Egyptian Hieroglyphs for Beginners $28.95**

MUSIC BASED ON THE PRT M HRU AND OTHER KAMITAN TEXTS

Available on Compact Disc $14.99

Music of Ancient Egypt
By
Sebai Maa
(Muata Ashby)

The Music of Ancient Egypt collection is an exploration of ancient Egyptian musical forms and concepts using ancient Egyptian musical instrument reproductions to discover the mysteries of Kemetic (ancietn Egyptian) devotional musical feeling. The fruit of years of research have given fruit to a unique sound and musical conception which at times sounds ancient and at other times fuses Ancient Egyptian feeling with modern writhyms of the world including West African, Middle Eastern, Soul, Jazz, and East Indian styles. Using authentic the Ancient Egyptian words derived from inscriptions, hymns and papyri such as the Ancient Egyptian Book of the Dead, a wonderful and special musical vision has emerged. A must for lovers of Ancient Egyptian culture and mysticism and alternative music.

©1999 **Muata Ashby**

Adorations to the Goddess

**Music for Worship of the Goddess
NEW Egyptian Yoga Music CD
by Sehu Maa**

By Sehu Maa (Muata Ashby)
Based on the Words of Power of Ra and Hetheru
played on reproductions of Ancient Egyptian Instruments **Ancient Egyptian Instruments used: Voice, Clapping, Nefer Lute, Tar Drum, Sistrums, Cymbals – The Chants, Devotions, Rhythms and Festive Songs Of the Neteru – Ideal for meditation, and devotional singing and dancing.**
©1999 By Muata Ashby
CD $14.99 –
UPC# 761527100221

SONGS TO OSIRIS ASET AND HERU
NEW
Egyptian Yoga Music CD
By Sehu Maa
played on reproductions of Ancient Egyptian Instruments– **The Chants, Devotions, Rhythms and**
Festive Songs Of the Neteru - Ideal for meditation, and devotional singing and dancing.
Based on the Words of Power of Asar (Osiris), Aset (Aset) and Heru (Heru) Om Asar Aset Heru is the third in a series of musical explorations of the Kamitan (Ancient Egyptian) tradition of music. Its ideas are based on the Ancient Egyptian Religion of Osiris, Aset and Heru and it is designed for listening, meditation and worship. ©1999 By Muata Ashby
CD $14.99 –
UPC# 761527100122

HAARI OM: ANCIENT EGYPT MEETS INDIA IN MUSIC
NEW Music CD
By Sehu Maa

The Chants, Devotions, Rhythms and
Festive Songs Of the Ancient Egypt and India, harmonized and played on
reproductions of ancient instruments along with modern instruments and beats.
Ideal for meditation, and devotional singing and dancing.
Haari Om is the fourth in a series of musical explorations of the Kamitan
(Ancient Egyptian) and Indian traditions of music, chanting and devotional
spiritual practice. Its ideas are based on the Ancient Egyptian Yoga spirituality
and Indian Yoga spirituality.
©1999 By Muata Ashby
CD $14.99 –UPC# 761527100528

RA AKHU: THE GLORIOUS LIGHT
NEW
Egyptian Yoga Music CD
By Sehu Maa
The fifth collection of original music compositions based on the Teachings and
Words of The Trinity, the God Osiris and the Goddess Nebethet, the Divinity

Aten, the God Heru, and the Special Meditation Hekau or Words of Power of Ra from the Ancient Egyptian Tomb of Seti I and more...
played on reproductions of Ancient Egyptian Instruments and modern instruments - **Ancient Egyptian Instruments used: Voice, Clapping, Nefer Lute, Tar Drum, Sistrums, Cymbals**
– The Chants, Devotions, Rhythms and Festive Songs Of the Neteru – Ideal for meditation, and devotional singing and dancing.
©1999 By Muata Ashby
CD $14.99 –Cassette $10
UPC# 761527100825

GLORIES OF THE DIVINE MOTHER
Based on the hieroglyphic text of the worship of Goddess Net.
The Glories of The Great Mother
©2000 **Muata Ashby**
CD $14.99 UPC# 761527101129

DUA ASAR

Special songd dedicated to Asar based on the Hymn to Asar in the Prt M Hru Text

©2005 **Muata Ashby**
CD $19.99

Udja,

This CD includes songs from the year 2003-2005 including the new song that was played for the attendees at the 2005 Summer Neterian Conference is now completed and will be available beginning September 1.

This song is the first to be completed by Sebai Maa that incorporates the English language along with the Kemetic and constitutes a milestone in musical production. It is dedicated to the Divine in the form of Om and Amun Ra Ptah. The cover is a painting by Sebai Maa to represent the impetus of the music.

CD Live Performance – Recorded at the Year 2000 Goddess Festival
Contains the chants of the goddess accompanied by hand drumming, sistrum, cymbals and clapping.
CD $14.99
©2000 **Muata Ashby**

CD Kemetic Meditation
Contains compilation of music especially ordered for meditative practice and relaxation accompanied by Nefer

Ancient Egyptian guitar, drumming, sistrum, cymbals and clapping.
CD $14.99
©2000 **Muata Ashby**

NEFER: "THAT WHICH IS BEAUTIFUL": The Music of the Ancient Egyptian Lute (Guitar)
Volume 1
for Relaxation and Meditation
by Seba Maa
UPC# 761527100924
CD-$14.99–©1999 Muata Ashby

Order Form

Telephone orders: Call Toll Free: 1(305) 378-6253. Have your AMEX, Optima, Visa or MasterCard ready.

Fax orders: 1-(305) 378-6253   E-MAIL ADDRESS: Semayoga@aol.com

Postal Orders: Sema Institute of Yoga, P.O. Box 570459, Miami, Fl. 33257. USA.

Please send the following books and / or tapes.

ITEM

_____Cost $_____

_____Cost $_____

_____Cost $_____

Total $_____

Name:_____

Physical Address:_____

City:_____ State:_____ Zip:_____

Sales tax: Please add 6.5% for books shipped to Florida addresses

_____Shipping: $6.50 for first book and .50¢ for each additional

_____Shipping: Outside US $5.00 for first book and $3.00 for each additional

_____Payment:_____

_____Check -Include Driver License #:

_____Credit card: _____ Visa, _____ MasterCard,

_____ AMEX.

Card number:_____

Name on card:_____ Exp.

____date:_____/_____

Copyright 1995-2006 Sema Institute of Yoga
P.O.Box 570459, Miami, Florida, 33257
(305) 378-6253 Fax: (305) 378-6253